CONTENTS

KU-498-694

FOREWORD

When I started my first NVQ, in Business Administration, it was my opportunity to gain a national qualification while working. Busy days of paperwork were converted into performance criteria and knowledge bases, which are the foundation of NVQs. My success with Business Administration led me to do NVQ's in Customer Care and Information and Library Services.

NVQ's are best practice and competence-based national qualifications that recognize staff talents and skills. Industry likes them as they show that their employees are competent in their work. In this book NVQs are clearly and expertly explained by Hazel Dakers. Her deep understanding and knowledge of competence-based training enables her to explain how to achieve these qualifications. For both employer and employee, Hazel Dakers sets out what is required in clear and concise English. Her unwavering support for competence-based qualifications covers all sectors of industry.

I have gained so much confidence, knowledge and four different qualifications from my NVQs. I continue to work and support the ethos of NVQs and heartily endorse them. This book will show anyone how to start, regardless of age or academic ability, to become more competent in his or her work.

Jim Jackson
February 2002

3rd edition

NVQs
& how to
get them

WITHDRAWN

hazel dakers

*With thanks to the family, colleagues
and other friends who stood by me during 1995*

First published in 1996
Second edition published in 1998
Third edition published in 2002

Kogan Page Limited
120 Pentonville Road
London N1 9JN

© Hazel Dakers, 1996, 1998, 2002

British Library Cataloguing in Publication Data

A CIP record for this book is available from the British Library.

ISBN 0 7494 3711 1

Typeset by Jean Cussons Typesetting, Diss, Norfolk
Printed and bound in Great Britain by Clays Ltd, St Ives plc

WHY A THIRD EDITION?

I was delighted to hear that Kogan Page considered this little book had been sufficiently in demand to warrant a third edition. I was encouraged still further to come across readers who have found it helpful. Then came the daunting task. During the three and a half years since *NVQs and How to Get Them* was last published, NVQs have been changing quite a lot. Organizations themselves have also been changing and a new administrative structure is being introduced by government during 2002. This is of less direct importance to you as a candidate – provided that you know where to go for information.

The third edition has required the replacement of approximately one quarter of the second edition. NVQs have not simply settled down but they have become ensconced at the centre of vocational training in the UK. By March 2001 more than 3 million certificates had been awarded.

Around NVQs are now established Foundation and Advanced Modern Apprenticeships which, in addition to an NVQ, have other segments to make them even more rounded training experiences. Modern Apprenticeships include Key Skills and sometimes Technical Certificates.

NVQs themselves have become more flexible. An NVQ may be written in many styles providing it still expresses the requirements of a worker to the national standard in a particular field. There is no automatic format to expect as there used to be.

Vocationally Related Qualifications, linked with NVQs, are now in widespread use.

ACKNOWLEDGEMENTS

I would like to thank the standard-setting bodies and ITOs and their artists who have permitted the use of illustrations in this book since it was first published. They are: The Biscuit, Cake, Chocolate and Confectionery Alliance (BCCCA) and Barry Jackson, pages 20 and 101; BLC, The Leather Technology Centre, page 36; Management Charter Initiative (MCI), pages 6, 43 and 95; The Residential Estate Agency Training and Education Association (REATEA), page 2; and Periodicals Training Council (PTC), pages 4, 11, 17, 25 and 39. The *Evening Standard* was good enough to allow use of the illustration on page 58. The example of an element used throughout Chapter 8 is included with the kind permission of the Council for Administration, and that in Chapter 9 with the kind permission of British Ports Industry Training (BPIT).

I should like to thank Ann Harper of QCA for bringing me up to date on the recent changes in NVQs, Carla Harrison of CHNTO for her helpful comments and Phillip Mudd of Kogan Page for encouraging me to produce a third edition. Andrew and Chris Dakers have brought food and drink to my computer as I've sat rewriting sections of the book during weekends.

In particular I must thank Mary Fleming, Training Officer at Gateshead Libraries, Arts & Information Services, who has undertaken much of the research for this edition. She has also been an invaluable critic, urging me towards greater clarity for, as an experienced NVQ Programme Manager, she has her finger on the pulse of candidates' needs. Mary has also stopped me removing sections of the book that she has found useful with her own NVQ candidates.

INTRODUCTION

'Which is the book about NVQs we should all have on our library shelves?' I was asked at a meeting of senior public librarians. My response was that I should like to write it. So here it is.

If you have heard that an NVQ would be a good way to further your career and you wonder how and why, this is a straightforward explanation of NVQs and how to get them. The subject is usually, though quite unnecessarily, veiled in mystery. NVQs are for everyone and so everyone should be able to find out easily how to acquire them. This book sets out to help you do just that.

Books abound on the theory and concepts of competence, work-based learning, functional analysis and the different means of assessment. I touch on these issues but only to the extent that you need to understand them to get an NVQ.

As a driver I know I have to put petrol in my car, but I make no attempt to understand its construction or maintenance needs. I leave those things to the manufacturer and the service engineer. Similarly, I assume that the potential NVQ candidate will need to feel assured as to the quality of the qualification. The candidate needs to operate within the system in the same way as I need to operate my car.

I assure any Scottish readers that I am fully aware of the existence of SVQs. To simplify the book I have only referred to NVQs but in nearly every respect they are the same. Relevant Scottish abbreviations have been included, as have sources of information in Scotland, Wales and Northern Ireland.

By the end of this book I hope you will feel that the NVQ system is a well thought out and useful one. I hope you will be excited at the prospect of embarking on an NVQ, and that you will have enjoyed reading about how to get it.

1. WHAT IS AN NVQ?

⇨ Background

⇨ Definition

⇨ What's special about NVQs?

⇨ Competent and not yet competent

⇨ More useful facts about NVQs

⇨ Background

Is there a National Vocational Qualification (NVQ) for your kind of work? Almost certainly there is. More than 120 sets of NVQs have been developed to cover nearly every kind of work that people do in the UK. The 124 sets are divided into 11 very broad groups. NVQs are developed at five levels ranging from the quite straightforward at level 1 to the very complex at level 5. You will find the 124 sets of NVQs listed on pages 117–18 and the detail of the levels explained on pages 95–96.

The ideas for the NVQ system were first put forward in the mid-1980s. The main reason for devising what was then a new system was that as a country we were doing very badly compared with our economic rivals. The government noticed that our successful competitors had more highly qualified workforces in most occupations. It therefore decided that our future economic success probably depended upon better training and qualifications.

The government also discovered that in the UK we had a great variety of different kinds of qualification. Consequently employers looking for staff were unable to work out which applicants had the qualifications most suited to the job vacancy. So the government decided to draw up the NVQ Framework of 11 broad groups of NVQs at five levels within which all NVQs are placed. This NVQ Framework provides a basis to link with other national and international qualifications.

⇨ Definition

If you have a National Vocational Qualification (NVQ) it shows that you can do the work for which it has been awarded and do it to the *national standard*. This means that you are *competent* in this kind of work. For this reason NVQs are described as *competence-based qualifications*.

An NVQ *reflects* a typical kind of *job*. It will not be exactly the same as your particular job but it will be very much the same as a group of similar jobs.

The *best* place to be *checked* to see whether you have reached the standard of an NVQ, or a part of one, is *at work*. Only at work can it be seen that you carry out your job competently – to the national standard.

You may have to do some *training* before you are assessed. Some of this training may be away from your job, or you may find you do all of it at work.

DEFINITION

- An NVQ is a competence-based qualification
- An NVQ reflects the needs of the workplace
- An NVQ is best assessed in the workplace
- Achievement of an NVQ will often require training

⇨ What's special about NVQs?

You will read full examples of units of an NVQ in Chapters 8 and 9. Here, we will look at some of the special features of NVQs so that you can begin to see what makes them different from other qualifications.

NVQs state very clearly what has been done to carry out an activity competently. These results are listed in a very straightforward way. The list is called the Performance Criteria.

NVQs check whether you can carry out these Performance Criteria in a variety of different contexts. These contexts are called Range. If you have an NVQ to show that you work competently it will also show that you are competent in a whole lot of different situations.

NVQs show what you can do. However, in order to *do* it is often necessary also to *know*. This deeper understanding of what you are doing is called Underpinning Knowledge and Understanding.

If you have an NVQ to show that you are competent according to our national occupational standards it will show your abilities in three directions:

1. You will be able to carry out your work in most usual situations.
2. You will be able to carry out your work in a variety of different situations.
3. You will be able to carry out your work with understanding.

© MCI

SOME OF THESE SPECIAL FEATURES MAY BE IN YOUR NVQ

- NVQ elements containing Performance Criteria (results of actions taken)
- NVQ elements containing Range (contexts)
- NVQ elements containing Underpinning Knowledge and Understanding (UKU) (theory, principles)
- NVQs are sometimes expressed by entire unit rather than by element
- NVQs sometimes combine the factors listed above
- NVQs do not need to express Range separately

⇨ Competent and not yet competent

Thinking of school exam grades, do you realize that with our 'Cs', 'Ds', 'Es' and 'Fs' we passed well, quite well, not that well and only just! Which of those grades shows our abilities are of a good enough standard to do a job properly?

When NVQs were being devised it was decided to look at them in a different way. It seemed more sensible to first decide what are the criteria necessary to carry out a given job competently and then measure people against those criteria. In this way the standard would be even from year to year. This is called *criterion-referencing*.

National Vocational Qualifications are criterion-referenced. If you take NVQs you either do or do not match up to the standard or criteria. If you do match up you are assessed as *competent*. If you do not match up to the criteria you are assessed as *not yet competent*. You cannot be excellently competent, very competent, very nearly competent or half competent. Competence exists or does not yet exist!

You will already be used to this attitude if you have taken swimming certificates as a child, or the driving test. You are either safe to be let loose or you are not yet safe and can try the test again. No examiner is going to pass you for being half safe, I hope.

⇨ **More useful facts about NVQs**

NVQs cover 124 areas of work. The NVQ Framework links NVQs at all five levels, of which Level 1 is the lowest level of difficulty. (Chapter 13 tells you more about levels and there is a list of occupational areas on pages 117–18).

This should make it easier, once you are in the NVQ system, to move jobs. You will be able to show that what you have learnt in one job is valuable in another. You can enter the system at any point you have agreed with your assessor. In other words, to take a Level 3 there is no need first to achieve Levels 1 and 2. You can only register for the level at which you are working in your job. There is a description of NVQ levels on pages 95–96. As you will see, they go from quite junior to very senior jobs.

You can work through the units which make up an NVQ at your own pace. You do not have to spend a particular period studying before you are assessed. Your assessor will judge the evidence of what you can *do* – not what you have been *taught*.

THE NVQ SYSTEM

- The NVQ Framework covers 124 occupational areas
- The NVQ Framework covers five levels
- The NVQ system may be entered at any level
- NVQs are achieved by demonstrating work carried out to the national standard

PROGRESS LIST

This progress list is here to remind you what you will learn about NVQs in this book and what stage you have reached so far.

☑ What is an NVQ?

☐ Why take an NVQ?

☐ How to become an NVQ candidate

☐ What is an assessment centre?

☐ What does the assessor do?

☐ What does the candidate do?

☐ How to find your way around an NVQ

☐ Focus on an NVQ unit

☐ Spotlight on a very different NVQ unit

☐ The wider world of NVQs

☐ A portfolio?

☐ What next?

☐ The NVQ framework

☐ Persuading your boss about NVQs

Now you know what an NVQ is. Next you are going to look at the reasons why you may wish to register for an NVQ.

2. WHY TAKE AN NVQ?

⇨ Reasons

⇨ National standard of competence

⇨ Not the same as a course

⇨ No barriers to entry

⇨ Flexibility and transferability

⇨ NVQs and academic qualifications

⇨ Reasons

I expect you will be thinking of taking an NVQ for one of several reasons:

1. You are considering it because it is a leading qualification for work.
2. You want to prove to yourself and others just how able you are.
3. You think it will help you to progress in your career.

⇨ **National standard of competence**

NVQs can only be achieved through the demonstration of skills. Getting your NVQ will show that you have proved your abilities to the national standard. The national occupational standards express the way in which work may best be carried out now. They reflect best practice nationally, within Europe and internationally. If you work to those standards you are considered competent now. In terms of work, a qualification which proves that you can do your job competently must be a very valuable possession.

⇨ **Not the same as a course**

Have you noticed, the word 'course' has not yet been mentioned? NVQs are about far more than courses. After all, you can sit through hours, days, weeks or even years of a course and yet no one has any means of knowing what you have gained from it. And there is no proof that you can put the learning into practice. *NVQs show that you can* **do** *as well as know.*

It may be that to assist you with taking your NVQ you may take a course or two. A course may help you to fill in some gaps on matters of which you have only learnt a little on the job. In particular, courses may help you to acquire the Underpinning Knowledge and Understanding (UKU) – theory and principles – without which it is unlikely you will be competent. People need to know *why* they are doing things to do them well and *what* to do when things go wrong.

An NVQ is not proof that you can repeat what you learnt on a course. An NVQ is proof that your skills match the national standard of work performance.

NOT THE SAME AS A COURSE

An NVQ measures:

- Your ability to do and know
- Your underpinning knowledge and understanding
- Your formal and informal training
- Your formal and informal testing

⇨ No barriers to entry

You do not need any other formal qualification to allow you to work towards your NVQ. Nor do you need the level of NVQ below that which you now want to acquire. What you do need is to establish, usually with the help of your employer, which NVQ at what level best corresponds with the job you do. You can only be assessed for what you actually do.

You can put evidence towards your NVQ which you collected from working temporarily, part-time, full-time or voluntarily. People have obtained them through experimental projects based on unpaid work in the home.

Neither language nor disability nor age can pose a barrier to entry provided that the candidate is able to carry out the work to the national standard.

Training to the national standard is what NVQs are all about. You may learn in many ways: by being shown how to carry something out by a colleague or supervisor, by reading a book, by watching a video or by computer-assisted training. As far as NVQs are concerned, it does not matter how you acquired your skills as long as they are of the national standard.

NO BARRIERS TO NVQ ENTRY

- No prior qualification needed
- Language need not stop you
- Disability need be no barrier
- Age need not prevent you becoming an NVQ candidate

⇨ Flexibility and transferability

NVQs make your skills more transferable. That is, a skill you have acquired in one place through one activity can be taken with you to a different situation. You may not do book-keeping in your current job but you may do it as treasurer of your local football team or playgroup. Evidence from this hobby counts towards the NVQ (if it is an NVQ that includes some book-keeping). In turn the NVQ acts as proof that you can do book-keeping competently when you next apply for a job.

NVQs also demonstrate flexibility in using your skills. During your assessment you will exhibit your abilities in applications different from those with which you most usually work. You will demonstrate that you are flexible enough to adapt what is fundamentally the same activity working in a different context.

As time goes on it looks as though NVQs will have a future both as national and international currency for employment.

THE FLEXIBILITY AND TRANSFERABILITY OF NVQs

- Skills may be taken from one situation to another
- People are able to apply skills in different situations
- Value overseas

⇨ NVQs and academic qualifications

So, what is the special difference between NVQs and traditional qualifications?

Academic qualifications, GCSEs, A levels, degrees and so on, are awarded through the acquisition of a body of knowledge selected by an examination board, a group of teachers or lecturers. This knowledge is what these education providers consider to be a useful collection of learning. If you take one of these qualifications the success of your learning is tested either by assignment or by examination, or both. The practical examinations in subjects such as science, art and geography are simulated exercises designed to test learning but do not set out to prove capability for work. The learning is usually done in a prescribed way by following a course.

If you are awarded an NVQ this will be because you have achieved the outcomes (results of activities) identified as necessary to carry out an occupation. Many forms of evidence may be used to show that these outcomes have been reached and it does not matter how you have achieved them.

DIFFERENCES BETWEEN NVQs AND ACADEMIC QUALIFICATIONS

NVQs:
- Match nationally identified needs for work
- Make use of many forms of evidence and are assessed in many ways

Academic qualifications:
- Are based on topics selected by course providers
- Are tested by assignment and/or exam

SELF-ASSESSMENT CHECKLIST

Please complete this self-assessment checklist to help decide if an NVQ might be right for you. Do you want:

	Yes	No
to be qualified as competent at your work?	☐	☐
to take a qualification without having to take a course?	☐	☐
to have an opportunity to qualify whoever you are, no matter what your previous educational experience?	☐	☐
to have a qualification which proves your skills are transferable and towards which skills acquired anywhere may count?	☐	☐
to qualify to the national standards needed in your work rather than to those of providers of education and training?	☐	☐

If you answered 'Yes' to most of these questions, move on to the next chapter!

3. HOW TO BECOME AN NVQ CANDIDATE

⇨ Find an approved assessment centre

⇨ Awarding bodies

⇨ Initial assessment

⇨ Register for your NVQ

⇨ Use the services of the assessment centre

⇨ Find an approved assessment centre

There are several places to find out about a convenient approved assessment centre:

1. Your employer
2. Your local Learning and Skills Council (LSC)
3. The awarding body for NVQs in your field
4. The standard-setting body for your job

5. Your public library (see pp 112–13)
6. Your local careers office
7. Your local Next Step Shop

You may think it is difficult to find out through either the awarding body or the standard-setting body because you do not know which yours is. QCA (the Qualifications and Curriculum Authority) will be able to help you identify the right one (see 'Where to find out more' on page 110).

Candidates all have to register with an assessment centre. This will have been approved for the particular NVQ the candidate wishes to take.

Different assessment centres will offer different services to candidates. If you live or work in an area where there is a choice of assessment centres for your NVQ, find out what each one has to offer.

⇨ Awarding bodies

Some NVQs may be obtained from several different awarding bodies. The NVQ is worth exactly the same but you may be more used to the way one awarding body goes about its work than another. You could therefore find several assessment centres in your area approved for the same NVQ by different awarding bodies.

© PTC

There are a great many awarding bodies. Among the best known are City and Guilds, Edexel and OCR (Oxford Cambridge and RSA Examinations). In certain occupations, an awarding body has been chosen for its specialism within the particular field. All have to work to the same rules laid down by QCA (the Qualifications and Curriculum Authority).

⇨ Initial assessment

As you already know, there is no pre-entry requirement restricting the level at which you may enter the NVQ system. However, your work, upon which evidence you will be assessed, must include the activities to be assessed.

An initial assessment is essential to find the correct starting point. This might be a checklist you skim through on your own or with one of the centre staff. It might very well be carried out as an informal chat. If you are having a preliminary look for yourself, look at the contents of each unit of the qualifications in detail and then see which units go to make up which level of qualification. You know what your work is so you will have a very good idea of the NVQ level which is suitable for you.

At this point it is also likely that some gaps will be identified in your skills. Some element of planning to fill those gaps should come into play at this stage.

Those of you who have traditional qualifications already should consider this warning. You may be very highly qualified academically but that is not an automatic indication of your likely NVQ level. Your current job may not reflect the potential indicated by your academic qualification. The NVQ will be a useful further qualification which will demonstrate that not only do you *know* (which is provided by your academic qualification) but you can also *do*.

An initial assessment:

- Will help to find a starting point
- Will establish what your job includes
- Will explain why previous qualifications may be no indication of level

⇨ **Register for your NVQ**

This will be the first formal step you take towards getting an NVQ. You must be formally registered at least 10 weeks before you apply for certification. When you pay your registration fee to the assessment centre, you are committing yourself to qualifying as competent. This will cost between about £20 and £45 depending on the level and size of the NVQ. If you are lucky your employer will be paying as part of a staff development programme.

If you are paying for yourself check out whether you are eligible for any support scheme operating through your local Learning Skills Council. Check both where you live and where you work. Each region may choose its own funding priorities. *Money to Learn* (see p 113), a booklet also available on the Web, published by the Department for Education and Skills, lists any form of nationally available funding for adults obtaining Further Education and Training. (Special provision is made for 16–19 year olds, which is covered in *Financial Help for Students*, also published by DfES.) The Individual Learning Account mentioned in this booklet has recently been abolished. Part-time and distance learning students are eligible for Career Development Loans. For candidates taking college courses towards their NVQ it may be possible to obtain help from the Access Fund or Child Support Fund. Work-based Learning for Adults and the various ranges of New Deal are also explained as well as other sources of funding information.

The following chart will give you some idea of the range of prices for NVQs. However, the need to check your particular NVQ's costs can not be overstated.

Level	Range	Usual
2	£40–£120	£40–£50
3	£44–£170	£60–£70
4	£66–£200	£100–£120

Some awarding bodies allow staged payments which may ease the pain but may also turn out more costly overall. On average the additional cost will be:

Level	Additional cost
2	£10–£20
3	£15–£30
4	£20–£40

For example, it is possible to take this staged approach to Accounting Level 4. The candidate registration is £47. To this must be added 8 units at £8.65 each, totalling £116.20.

Awarding bodies arrange their charges by different methods and according to the particular NVQ. A rough guide to the total cost of taking an NVQ – excluding additional training or materials you may need – is £40 to £200. This will include registration, candidate record and standards or scheme book, assessment and certification.

REGISTER FOR YOUR NVQ

- Registration must be 10 weeks before certification
- Registration costs about £20–£50
- Total cost depends on level and size of NVQ, say £250–£500
- Sources of help:
  - Employer
  - Learning and Skills Council
  - *Money to Learn* booklet

⇨ Use the services of the assessment centre

Remember that you are the customer of a training and qualifications service. This service is being offered by the centre at which you have registered. Make sure, if there are alternative centres available, that you have selected the centre of greatest benefit to you.

Most will provide courses of one sort or another designed to help you fill those training gaps identified in your initial assessment. You will almost certainly have needed to commit yourself to the cost of this training – which is likely to have assessment built into it – as a requirement of registering with the centre.

These days, training is not only through traditional courses. It may well include an element of 'open learning'. This is largely an independent activity which is often focused upon the resources of a library/information centre or upon distance learning. Use any resources offered. The responsibility is very much with you as the candidate. If your employing organization has registered as a centre you will almost certainly have the opportunity for planned training on the job. The centre will provide at least one member of staff to whom you will have access for guidance. Be guided!

The centre may well arrange group meetings of candidates for mutual support and self-help. Take advantage of these. The NVQ system is intended to be tailored to the individual's needs. Make sure it is tailored to *your* needs.

Use your assessment centre to provide:

● Formal/informal gap-filling training
● Traditional courses
● Open/distance learning
● Support for planned learning on the job

But responsibility remains with the candidate supported by:
    centre staff
    other candidates

CHECKLIST: ACTION PLAN TO BECOME A CANDIDATE

Use this checklist to help you plan the steps you need to take to become an NVQ candidate.

(tick box when complete)

1. Find out what centres are convenient to you   ❏

2. Compare facilities   ❏

3. Compare fees   ❏

4. Investigate financial help   ❏

5. Select most suitable for you   ❏

6. Undergo initial assessment   ❏

7. Register for level advised   ❏

8. Use your assessment centre   ❏

4. WHAT IS AN ASSESSMENT CENTRE?

> ⇨ Definition
>
> ⇨ Where is an assessment centre?
>
> ⇨ Alternative types of assessment centre

⇨ Definition

An assessment centre is an organization rather than a physical place. In other words, an organization operating on several sites would still be one centre.

To become a centre, an organization has to comply with the rules of the awarding body. These rules are a reflection of the regulations established by QCA. All these regulations exist to ensure that you, the candidate, are assured quality and equivalence no matter at which centre you are registered.

Broadly speaking, your centre is expected to have certain resources, including management systems, suitably qualified and competent staff, adequate physical resources, and quality and assessment procedures. As in all other aspects of NVQs you will expect to find equality of opportunity and access.

To explain this in another way, you will expect to find a well-planned assessment programme with proper communication taking place between the staff involved. These staff will be qualified by the Employment NTO (or its successor SSC) to carry out their duties to the national standard and they will be designated competent in the occupational area for which you are being assessed. You will expect to find efficient records and regular monitoring for quality. QCA expects centres to make provision for special needs. You might wish to enquire about these arrangements when you are comparing centres.

DEFINITION OF AN ASSESSMENT CENTRE

An organization which complies with QCA regulations regarding:

● quality management systems
● qualified staff
● adequate physical resources
● quality assurance
● assessment services
● equality of opportunity
● open access

⇨ **Where is an assessment centre?**

If you work for a large organization and are lucky, your *employing organization* will be an approved assessment centre for the NVQ you want to take. As the evidence put towards the assessment for your NVQ will largely come from your job, a centre at your workplace is the one most likely to be tailored to the needs of your job. Equally it is far more likely that your boss will give you opportunities to widen your experience and cover all the necessary Range, if you are taking your NVQ at work. From the organization's point of view, the qualification will be seen as more closely answering its own needs.

If your employing organization is an assessment centre, it is most likely to match the training it organizes to the skills gaps which you need to fill to obtain your NVQ. An atmosphere will be more likely in which staff are expected to be constantly improving their skills. Support of many kinds will be given for self-improvement in the learning organization.

This kind of assessment centre will almost certainly be entirely financed by your employer. Your assessor might be your line manager or a member of staff from the training department.

Some employing organizations are just too small, or have too few staff of a particular occupation, for it to be worth their while becoming an assessment centre. Those who see the need for one closely linked with the workplace will sometimes join a *consortium assessment centre*. A group of organizations will cooperatively share assessment facilities. If you are being assessed through one of these centres you will have the additional interest of coming into contact with candidates and assessors from other similar organizations. Training arrangements may well be cooperative. Your assessor might still be your own line manager, but equally could come from another organization. Your employer is still almost certain to foot the bill.

Training and education providers may also become assessment centres. These could include your local college of further education, universities, independent (commercial) training organizations and the Learning and Skills Council. These organizations have viewed assessment as an additional service which will enhance their education and training provision.

Some NVQs will be more suited than others to assessment away from the job or *simulations* (mock-ups) of work situations. For this reason some assessment centres will be approved to cover certain units of an NVQ but not a whole one. Others will provide courses designed to provide only the *Underpinning Knowledge* towards an NVQ.

In some cases, assessors no longer usually working in your field will be expected to spend regular time back on the job to retain current occupational competence. This practical experience will ensure that they can still *do* what they are assessing and are not out of date.

Some candidates will use non-work-based centres individually, paying for themselves, and others will be sponsored by their employers.

Many of the same advantages and disadvantages will apply to *independent training providers* (such as commercial training organizations and other independent training institutions) as to colleges and universities. Some will have particularly strong links with certain industries or employing organizations and their smaller size may make them more flexible in matching your needs. On the other hand their smaller size may also result in fewer physical resources. More of the staff may spend part of their time practising their occupation as well as teaching it. They may appear to have less monitoring of their training activities than a college – but remember they will have to be good to stay in business. Payment may be by you or your employer.

WHERE IS A SUITABLE ASSESSMENT CENTRE?

- At work?
- A consortium of linked organizations?
- The local FE college?
- A nearby university?
- The local Learning and Skills Council?
- A specialist independent training provider?

PROGRESS LIST

This progress list reminds you of what you will learn about NVQs in this book and what stage you have reached so far.

☑ What is an NVQ

☑ Why take an NVQ?

☑ How to become an NVQ candidate

☑ What is an assessment centre?

☐ What does the assessor do?

☐ What does the candidate do?

☐ How to find your way around an NVQ

☐ Focus on an NVQ unit

☐ Spotlight on a very different NVQ unit

☐ The wider world of NVQs

☐ A portfolio?

☐ What next?

☐ The NVQ framework

☐ Persuading your boss about NVQs

Now let's take a look at what the key people do.

ALTERNATIVES TYPES OF ASSESSMENT CENTRE

	FOR	AGAINST
Work/consortium	1. Fits closely with job, internal career structure 2. Employer supportive towards learner – attitudes, training 3. Assessor really understands what is being assessed as works there too 4. Employer pays	1. May seem too narrow a learning experience 2. May not wish to be assessed by direct boss or other senior staff 3. May feel less responsible for own development and more directed
FE college/university	1. Widens experience socially 2. Widens experience of occupation 3. Expect up-to-date ideas and learning methods 4. Employer may or may not pay	1. May seem remote from workplace 2. Mock-ups may be used 3. May not be approved to cover entire NVQ

ALTERNATIVE TYPES OF ASSESSMENT CENTRE contd.

	FOR	AGAINST
Independent training provider	1. May seem closer to workplace than college	1. Training (but not assessment) may feel less monitored than college
	2. Staff may also practise within occupation	2. Atmosphere may not have breadth of college
	3. Likely to be smaller organization	3. May not have equivalent physical resources as larger organization
	4. Has to be good to remain in business	4. Simulations may be used
	5. Smaller organization should be flexible	5. May not be approved to cover entire NVQ
	6. Employer may or may not pay	
	7. Expect up-to-date ideas and learning methods	

NB. All assessment centres have to achieve the same standards set by the awarding body and these are regularly monitored by the awarding body. If you have a choice of assessment centre, you will not so much be choosing between good and bad as between more or less personally suited to you.

5. WHAT DOES THE ASSESSOR DO?

⇨ Guides candidate

⇨ Interprets standards for candidate

⇨ Plans assessment with candidate

⇨ Carries out assessment

⇨ Completes assessment records

⇨ Is qualified in assessment

⇨ Is occupationally competent

⇨ Guides candidate

Your assessor will be your chief guide to the entire NVQ process. For most people the NVQ process itself is a whole new way of life. It is therefore necessary to have an expert guide.

You may be a candidate with little previous experience of training; or you may have experience mainly with traditional qualification systems. Either way, you will need to get your mind around the new NVQ approach.

The ideas behind the approach and the differences between NVQs and traditional qualifications have been explained in the first two chapters of this book. You might want to glance back at some of those listed points just to remind yourself.

Your assessor will remind you that you are being assessed to the national standard – for doing your work to the standard of best current practice. The evidence you collect to prove this will be largely taken from your work, and the qualification when completed will show that you have the necessary skills to carry out your job. The way that you are assessed will be a lot less formal than an examination and you and your assessor will agree the pace at which you should take the NVQ.

⇨ Interprets standards for candidate

When you start to prepare towards your NVQ you will be introduced to a new style of English! When the NVQ system started it was considered important that all NVQs be written in a standardized way. There is now a mixture of styles of writing NVQs. Many of them you will find a little strange but the language of others is much easier to follow.

You will also need to become accustomed to interlinking the parts of a standard to make them fit together. Once you have been shown by your assessor how to do this for the first few standards, the style will become obvious and you will be able to do it for yourself. However, there will be occasions when you are not absolutely certain what the standard requires. At these times your assessor is the interpretation expert whose skills are available to you.

Assessor interprets standards for candidate

- Explains NVQ style of writing
- Shows how sections of standard must be interlinked
- Clarifies anything about which the candidate is unsure

⇨ Plans assessment with candidate

The assessor will look with you at how many units there are in the NVQ you want to take. Together you will probably prepare an outline plan covering all the stages of the NVQ. You will plan in more detail the first parts on which you have chosen to be assessed.

You will arrange which kinds of evidence will be assessed for the different activities, how much evidence you will need to produce and how you will arrange it. Naturally you will also arrange mutually convenient times for the assessment – which should always be pre-arranged and should never be a 'spot check'.

The plan need not be anything sophisticated or complicated. It can be a straightforward list of which each of you has a copy with dates jotted down by each stage of the process.

Assessor plans assessment with candidate including:

- outline plan – can be a simple list
- early stages in detail
- types of evidence
- how much evidence
- arrangement of evidence
- assessment times – no spot checks

⇨ Carries out assessment

Special assessment guidance notes are an integral part of each NVQ element. Both you, the candidate, and your assessor will use these in the planning process and they will remain a constant source of reference. There are no nasty hidden surprises in NVQs!

There are two kinds of evidence: *performance evidence* and *supplementary evidence*. Performance evidence is the preferred kind as it comes directly from the work itself. It may be that your assessor observes you carrying out some activities or that you present samples of your work as evidence. The amount of performance evidence is laid down in the standard.

Supplementary evidence is rather more indirect which is why it is not the preferred option. It may take the form of informal questioning or verbal or written tests of underpinning knowledge and understanding. You might write a report on something you have done or arrange that a colleague should provide a report as a witness.

You and your assessor have a variety of assessment tools at your disposal. With new-style NVQs, additional quality assurance has been introduced. This could be independent assessment of a part of each NVQ, which is being encouraged to control the assessment more rigorously. Independent assessment is likely to be in the form of written tests marked centrally by someone not known to the candidate. It may also include independent reviewing of your evidence, for which you will visit a registered centre or a visiting assessor will come to you. Or perhaps you will write a case study for assessment by an assessor not known to you. The assessor will look at all the evidence you present and weigh up whether your work yet matches up to the NVQ standard.

Assessor carries out the assessment looking at:

● Performance evidence:
  observation
  work samples
  reports
● Supplementary evidence:
  informal questioning
  verbal tests
  written tests
  witness report

and decides whether your evidence matches the standard

⇨ Completes assessment records

Because NVQs are very significant national qualifications, recording entitlements to them must be carried out very thoroughly. If this were not the case anyone could say they had an NVQ and you might not think it was worth getting one.

Your assessor will usually be concerned with two main forms of assessing you. Usually the assessor will sign one form to indicate your completion of an element and another when you have completed a unit (a set of elements). At the point when the internal verifier (who coordinates and supervises the assessors) checks that the assessor has carried out his/her work properly, the unit form will be countersigned. Within five weeks of completing a unit you should receive a certificate if you wish.

Assessor completes assessment records including:

- Form for element (not all new-style NVQs)
- Form for unit
- Recommends application for unit certificate

⇨ Is qualified in assessment

The people mainly responsible for running a system based on standards have to be up to standard themselves. Naturally enough, competence-based qualifications have also been developed for assessment and verification. These were drawn up by the Employment NTO (the organization representative of the employment occupational sector then responsible for NVQ development).

Your assessor will be qualified to 'assess candidate performance' (D32) and to 'assess candidate using differing sources of evidence' (D33). The internal verifier at your assessment centre will additionally be qualified to 'internally verify the assessment process' (D34). Once you have your NVQ in your chosen occupation, you, too, might wish to qualify as an assessor.

The assessor and internal verifier are qualified in assessment with these NVQ units:

- Assessor
  D32 Assess candidate performance
  D33 Assess candidate using differing sources of evidence
- Internal verifier:
  D34 Internally verify the assessment process

⇨ **Is occupationally competent**

It seems fairly obvious that if you are being assessed in, for instance, an agricultural occupation, you will not want to be assessed by someone who is qualified in assessment but is an expert in catering! An assessor must therefore be competent in the occupation that she or he is assessing. The standards-setting body will have a clear definition of occupational competence but it should be borne in mind that it will vary from one area of work to another.

MAITLAND . . . . .

MEMORY JOGGER

Don't forget:

Your assessor is your guide
Your assessor will explain the standards to you
Your assessment is planned jointly between you and your assessor
Your assessor looks at evidence of your competence
Your assessor completes assessment records
Your assessor is expert both in your occupation and in assessment

6. WHAT DOES THE CANDIDATE DO?

> ⇨ Takes responsibility for the overall process
>
> ⇨ Plans assessment with assessor
>
> ⇨ Undertakes training to fill gaps
>
> ⇨ Gathers evidence
>
> ⇨ Organizes evidence

⇨ Takes responsibility for the overall process

As an NVQ candidate you will find that you are responsible for your own training and qualifications. Whether you have been offered the opportunity at work to take an NVQ or sought the opportunity elsewhere, it is yours to take and yours to organize.

You move the process forward after registration by taking advantage of any opportunities offered. Such assistance may be in the form of a mentor (an experienced adviser or guide) in addition to your assessor, or assistance with formal or informal training. Your assessment centre should be able to give you at least informal information concerning support services available.

As the person in overall charge of your NVQ, you will need to make sure that all the others concerned in some way with you as a candidate are both consulted and kept informed about what you are doing. When your line manager is not your assessor this is all the more important. The line manager's cooperation in evidence collection, assessment by observation and secondment to necessary training will be essential. The line manager who is kept in the dark cannot be expected to cooperate.

THE CANDIDATE TAKES THE LEAD

- Takes responsibility
- Takes advantage of opportunities offered
- Liaises with all involved

⇨ Plans assessment with assessor

An assessment plan need not be anything very grand or complicated.

Common sense will tell you, however, that if two people are going to work on something together intermittently, they are going to have to agree:

1. when they will do it, and
2. what they will do on each occasion.

So, the assessment plan is likely to include a couple of initial meetings to ensure complete understanding of the standards being assessed, and to agree the likely kinds of evidence that the candidate will need to collect. Some observation sessions may need to be booked and dates agreed by which particular stages will be reached. It could usefully be set out as a plan and assessment diary. The planning information might be held in one column while another contains a record of what took place at each point on the plan. Above all you should consider this planning as a negotiation between you and your assessor as partners in the NVQ process.

⇨ Undertakes training to fill gaps

You probably don't see much point in taking a qualification that only confirms that what you do, you do well. An NVQ does more than confirm your current skills. New skills augmenting those you already possess are also certificated in an NVQ. The result should be that you may either expand your current job role or apply for other jobs with more scope. This is the pay-off for the extra effort to acquire those new skills.

Earlier in this book, it was explained that training for NVQs need not be through traditional courses. You may find that a colleague is in an ideal position to teach you how to carry out an activity which forms part of your NVQ unit. On the other hand it may be that what you need to learn can be conveniently found in a book or video presentation. If this is the case read or watch it and then try applying what you have learnt. Rather more formal ways of filling these gaps may be open or distance learning packages which could include booklets, videos, audio tapes, articles and CD ROMs or computer programs. Some NVQs attract a great many candidates because they apply to a significant part of the working population. These may have learning packages particularly matched to their units. The quality will vary and you may need the expert assistance of a trainer or librarian to select worthwhile material.

DIFFERENT WAYS OF TRAINING

- On the job with colleagues
- From book/video
- By open/distance learning course
- By traditional training course

The luckiest candidates will have training opportunities offered to them through their place of work. If you are one of these, your personnel or training department will have vetted the course offered. If you have to do this for yourself simply treat it as any other product and make some careful enquiries before you sign up – particularly if it is costing a good deal and is going to take up a lot of your time. It's always worth asking to speak to someone who has already been on the course.

You will want to make sure that the content is a close match with the NVQ units you plan to take. You may want to see what other facilities the organization offers to support your learning – a good library or learning resources centre, for example. How many people will attend each class? How much individual help will you be offered? Does the timing suit the rest of your life? In the end you may have to weigh up a course at one place with a good library and a large class, or a course at another with no library but smaller numbers of students. Only you know which will suit you best.

However you choose to acquire those additional skills, remember it is not numbers of books you have read or hours sat in courses that are being assessed. You will be assessed on your application of what you have learnt. To this extent any books, videos, trainers or colleagues who have helped you learn are being assessed with you. If you apply what you have learnt competently, it suggests that not only you but those who helped you with your training are also competent.

Before signing up for a course ask a former student/trainee:

- Was it value for money?
- Was it worth the time spent?
- Was it a good match with your NVQ units?
- How good were the support facilities?
- How big was the class?
- Was there much individual help?

Then consider whether the times are convenient for you

⇨ Gathers evidence

The evidence you collect will fall into two main categories: *performance* and *supplementary evidence*. It may come in any form – written, oral or visual. You are likely to be mainly concerned with the collection of performance evidence, as supplementary evidence will largely be questioning of one sort or another. Now NVQs will contain an additional layer of quality assurance. This will often comprise independent assessment for part of the NVQ. It is too early to say how this will work out, but it may include independent reviewing of your evidence, old-fashioned tests or multiple-choice questions.

Visual evidence does not have to mean your assessor standing there observing your work. However, this is likely to form some part of the overall assessment. Visual evidence may include photos and videos. Oral evidence could mean your assessor listening to you at work but is equally likely to be a cassette you have recorded yourself. Written evidence may be a report, a memo, a form that has to be completed as a regular part of your job or a report from a colleague or customer about how you have carried out a particular piece of work.

Let me provide a few more examples of the kinds of evidence you might collect – varying according to the type of work you do. Perhaps you record statistics, keep records for your organization, keep details of activities within a diary, prepare or contribute to the preparation of budgets or send letters. Many of these will support the units for which you are trying to prepare. Then again you may deal with work schedules, booking systems, flow charts, plans or layouts. You may have examples of administrative procedures you have helped to set up or operate.

In most jobs, provided that your line manager knows what you are doing, there is unlikely to be a problem in copying sufficient of these kinds of material for your evidence.

People do not always think of many of the things they do at work as providing performance or supplementary evidence, and yet they do. A list of the order in which you deliver meals on wheels, with timings, is a work schedule. A leave book that you keep for the department is an administrative procedure. The movement records of livestock that you complete if you work on a farm will count as statistics collection and record-keeping.

Twenty-five photos of you with your prize herd of cattle or the happy children in your playgroup will provide no more evidence than one photograph. There is a temptation to feel that the more you show of something, the more believable it is.

Two or three witness reports of your helpful switchboard management should suggest that it is not a rare occurrence for you to be polite and efficient on the telephone, especially if each describes a different situation requiring both tact and persistence. However, 10 statements to the effect that you are always efficient and helpful, with no detail, will tell the assessor next to nothing. Evidence must be substantiated so that it may be weighed up as in a court of law.

One telephone message or memo may well provide evidence of several different elements or contribute to the evidence for several different units. Economy with evidence will be applauded, not penalized. It indicates both clear thinking and efficiency. The assessment will be much easier for you and your assessor if you are economical

© MCI

with your evidence. Do not feel obliged to wheel your evidence to your assessor in a supermarket trolley!

⇨ Organizes evidence

Just imagine for a moment that your evidence is heaped up in the supermarket trolley. You have done a good job collecting everything you can think of. What should you do to make it a reasonable selection for your assessor to look at?

You will have to divide it into sections and arrange it so that it is easy for the assessor to look up and find particular items. If some pieces of evidence are supporting several activities you will need to provide links, or cross-references, between the evidence and the various elements to which they refer. (For more on organizing evidence, see Chapter 11.)

Further facts for candidates

● Competent candidate implies competent training
● Evidence must be substantiated
● Evidence should be economical
● Evidence should be well organized

SELF-ASSESSMENT

To establish if you are willing to take on the responsibilities of being an NVQ candidate, please complete the following self-assessment checklist.

	Yes	No
Do you want to be in charge of your own career development?	❑	❑
Do you want to plan your own qualifying process in partnership with your assessor?	❑	❑
Are you willing to seek out opportunities to advance your own training?	❑	❑
Would you find it interesting to collect evidence to prove just how competent you are?	❑	❑
Would you find it a challenge to organize that evidence so that it may be assessed easily?	❑	❑

If you answered 'Yes' to most of these questions, then it is time you found out more about what this NVQ actually looks like. So, take a look at the next chapter!

7. HOW TO FIND YOUR WAY AROUND AN NVQ

⇨ The changing look of NVQs

⇨ Aspects of NVQs

⇨ Core units

⇨ Optional units

⇨ Common units

⇨ Functions not tasks

⇨ NVQs and compliance

⇨ Languages other than English

⇨ The changing look of NVQs

Traditionally most NVQs are divided into units. Each of these units covers one of the main functions of the job roles of the typical candidate. Some NVQ units are further sub-divided into elements which in turn may be broken down into performance criteria. There may be several interwoven strands within these.

Now, however, there is a clear move away from extensive sub-division within NVQs and, instead, a move towards a stronger focus upon NVQ units (ie less detail).

Similarly, the way NVQs are written is changing. Many candidates feel the older-style NVQs contain too much jargon, and they find the stilted form in which they are written quite difficult to understand. Newer-style NVQs tend to be presented in clear everyday terms so that the people for whom they are written can understand them. Older-style NVQs also tend to be written in the passive form, for example, *'Information that will help your customer is quickly located'*. Newer-style NVQs use an active and much more personalized voice, for example, *'You need to show that you quickly locate information that will help your customer'*[1].

NVQs are:

- Usually divided into units
- Sometimes divided into elements
- Sometimes further sub-divided into performance criteria

⇨ Aspects of NVQs

All NVQs have titles and levels which help you to choose the right one for you. For example, Customer Services Level 2 or Information Technology Level 3. Most NVQs have units. These units, whether they make it obvious or not, will expect candidates to demonstrate that they can carry out the relevant functions across a range of contexts. For example, if candidates are required to 'demonstrate effective communication', the range of situations in which they need to do this will probably include: face-to-face, in writing or by telephone. Sometimes the contexts or 'range' will be spelt out and sometimes not.

---

[1] Institute of Customer Service, 2 Castle Court, St Peter's Street, Colchester, Essex CO1 1EW, Tel: 01206 571 716, enquiries@instanstserv.com, www.ics-nto.com.

Candidates are also required to demonstrate essential knowledge (sometimes called underpinning knowledge and understanding) of the particular area of work, in situations for which they are unable to provide evidence on the job. For example, a real emergency with all the danger this could create will not be triggered for an NVQ assessment! However, a fire drill might form part of an assessment and this might be supplemented by answers to assessor-set questions, or through special assignments to prove the candidate's knowledge. Sometimes the knowledge required will be clearly listed and sometimes not. Increasingly, as we will see in Chapter 10, Technical Certificates will become available that will provide a neat and separately packaged means of ensuring coverage of the required Knowledge. It may, for example, be possible to find a course which covers this at your local college or through *learndirect*, even if you do not obtain assessment through that course for your entire NVQ.

NVQs have:

- Titles
- Levels

NVQs expect:

- Performance in a variety of contexts
- Performance based on essential knowledge

⇨ Core units

There has been increasing recognition that many core skills are common to a good many occupations or associated occupations. These are represented in an NVQ as core, mandatory or common units.

In some areas of work being unable to competently carry out certain functions could be considered unprofessional. In other occupations it is the soft skills, such as providing high-quality customer service, which are considered core. This is why in order to obtain a particular NVQ there will be some units that you must take and in which you must be assessed as competent.

⇨ **Optional units**

At the same time it has been realized that in some respects the workforce becomes increasingly specialized. As life, including work, becomes more and more complex, so it becomes necessary for some people to specialize in the fine detail of just a few technical areas of an occupation. No single person will need that degree of detailed skill in all aspects and so the NVQ candidate is able to select relevant areas in which to be assessed in specialisms. These are shown in NVQs as optional units. You will need to work out which are the most suitable ones for you to take in consultation with your assessor and perhaps your line manager.

If you have difficulty in finding enough options for assessment in which you are sufficiently skilled, this probably means that your experience in your work is rather narrow. In this case, to complete your NVQ you will need to ask to rotate with colleagues and gain wider experience. You will also need to find and undertake the relevant training to be able to carry out your new activities competently.

The whole intention behind NVQs was to increase the skills of the UK national workforce. Not only does this mean increasing the level and quality to which people work but it also means increasing the breadth across which people are able to work competently. It is this breadth of experience and competence which enables people to move flexibly between jobs according to the skills for which there is a need. This is one of the reasons why your NVQ will help you to find jobs.

⇨ **Common units**

If you have already taken one NVQ you may recognize some units from it within the NVQ for which you are currently preparing evidence. Until recently, these borrowed units have always been identical. Now it is possible to tailor these units so that they are better matched to the new NVQ which has adopted them. Tailored or not, providing that the unit is common to both your NVQs – and not merely similar – your evidence towards the NVQ is simply your previous certificate for the unit.

NVQs may have:

● Optional units
● Mandatory units
● Common units

⇨ **Functions not tasks**

NVQ units describe functions. Functions usually have a number of tasks within them.

If you think of a domestic activity such as preparing a drink, which is familiar and straightforward, you will begin to realize that it includes a range of skills according to the type of drink being prepared. So the activity of preparing a drink is a *function*. On the other hand, in the preparation of a specific drink, instant coffee for example, a whole series of tasks must be carried out. These will include running the tap, putting water in the kettle, switching the kettle on, taking the lid off the jar of coffee and placing a spoonful of coffee in the mug. People often confuse functions and tasks.

NVQs are about functions which are fairly complex groups of activities describing their purpose and result. The function of preparing a drink is a complete activity seen through from beginning to end with a clear purpose and result. Too much attention to the detailed tasks of running the tap or boiling the water could lead to these being seen as ends in themselves, forgetful of the real purpose which is preparing a drink. We all know people who seem to run round in circles so absorbed in the detail of what they are doing that they no longer seem to know why they are doing it!

⇨ **NVQs and compliance**

NVQs include statutory/legal, environmental, health and safety requirements. Examples might include data protection, restrictions on harmful emissions or wearing protective clothing.

While the intentions behind NVQs are the same now as they were before, their appearance is far less standardized than it used to be. They still focus on the outcomes of work but, in a sense, look towards its larger goals more than the steps to achieve them.

The following two chapters provide examples of current NVQ units from the Council for Administration and from the British Ports Industry Training Board. These are Receive and Assist Visitors and Controlling Vehicle Movements. Each of these is written in the form of units and elements but the ways in which they are expressed and are laid out varies somewhat after this.

Bear in mind that it is always possible that your chosen NVQ may look more different still. Perhaps, for example, it will only have units. Regardless of its form it will still have within it the main functions of your job, the vital knowledge needed to do it and the varying contexts in which you may need to apply your skills and knowledge. Your assessment centre and, in particular your assessor, will provide the guidance you need and you can also contact your Sector Skills Council (SSC) through the Sector Skills Development Agency (SSDA), whose details are listed at the end of this book.

NVQs:

- Describe functions – not tasks
- Include compliance
- Vary in style as well as content

⇨ Languages other than English

Such has been the success of NVQs that there has been demand for them from candidates in countries beyond the UK. Under the new regulations your assessment may be in the language of the country in which you are assessed providing this is noted on your certificate.

If you are assessed in the UK in a language other than English or Welsh you must provide evidence that you are also capable in either English or Welsh to the level required to carry out your work competently anywhere in the UK.

As implied above, it is becoming increasingly possible to be assessed in Welsh or in 50 per cent English and 50 per cent Welsh. As demand increases so will facilities.

OTHER LANGUAGES

Assessment possible:

- In other countries and languages
- In other languages in the UK – if also competent in English or Welsh
- In Welsh

MEMORY JOGGER

Don't forget:

NVQs have titles and levels

NVQs expect compliance

NVQs require performance in different contexts

NVQs require performance based on knowledge

NVQs vary in style but usually have units

Some units will be mandatory

Usually some units will be optional

And some units will be common

8. FOCUS ON AN NVQ UNIT

⇨ Introduction to the NVQ unit

⇨ Standard to which you must work

⇨ Context (scope) in which you must work to standard

⇨ Knowledge needed to achieve standard

This NVQ/SVQ publication makes reference to the National Occupational Standards for Administration developed by the Council for Administration (CfA), which is the government-approved body representing the sector of Administration. For further information contact: The CfA, 18/20 Bromell's Road, London SW4 0BG. Tel (020) 7627 9876, www.cfa.uk.com.

Note: The author's commentary is in italics.

⇨ **Introduction to the NVQ unit**

The scene is set in which this section or unit of an NVQ will take place. It has two sub-sections or elements. It is suited to someone whose work includes reception duties.

Unit 212 Receive and assist visitors

About this unit

This unit is about providing a reception service to visitors.

You have to do two things:

212.1 Receive visitors
212.2 Assist visitors

Target group

This unit is for you if you have reception duties as part of your job.

NVQs and SVQs

This unit is an optional unit in the Administration NVQ/SVQ at Level 2. The scope for NVQ/SVQ assessment is shown on each page of the unit. For more information on interpreting these please see the Assessment Guidance document produced by the CfA.

⇨ **Standard to which you must work**

Clearly listed are all the actions you must always take to work to the national standard in your reception duties. If you think about it, each of these actions is one which you would wish to be taken by someone receiving you at their place of work.

⇨ **Context (scope) in which you must work**

This makes it clear that your actions must be the same whether the visitor appears easy or difficult. You must also treat visitors in the same way regardless of whether they come from another department within your organization or whether they have come from elsewhere. This section is placed alongside the standard to emphasize that the two work hand in hand. Note the scope or context is the same for both elements provided.

Unit 212 Receive and assist visitors

Element 212.1

> **You must be able to:**
> **Receive visitors**

National standard of work

You must always:
1. Make sure you have all the necessary equipment and materials available and in good order.[1]
2. Make sure that you and your work area present a positive image of your organization.
3. Greet **visitors** in a friendly but polite manner, without unnecessary delay.

Scope

You must show:
In meeting the national standard of work you must show that you can:

1. Deal with three of the following types of visitors:
  a) internal to your organization
  b) external to your organization

[1] For example, telephone, visitors' book, electronic entry system, information materials, computer terminal, internal telephone directory.

4. Find out your **visitors'** identity and the purpose of their visit.
5. Follow your organization's security procedures.
6. Contact the person they have come to see promptly, provide them with clear information about the **visitor** and follow their instructions.
7. Make sure details of the visit have been recorded.[2]
8. Provide the **visitor** with any required identification and make sure they return it on departure.

c) expected visitors
d) unexpected visitors
e) hostile visitors

Explanations or examples of terms used:

Each organization will vary a little in terms of its precise equipment and the details considered necessary to note about each visitor. You may be able to list some of the differences between the examples below and your own situation.

---

[2] For example, time of arrival, name of their company, who they are visiting, time of departure and car registration.

⇨ **Standard to which you must work**

Clearly listed are all the actions you must always take to work to the national standard in your reception duties. If you think about it, each of these actions is one which you would wish to be taken by someone receiving you to their place of work.

⇨ **Context (scope) in which you must work**

This makes it clear that your actions must be the same whether the visitor appears easy or difficult. You must also treat visitors in the same way regardless of whether they come from another department within your organization or whether they have come from elsewhere. This section is placed alongside the standard to emphasize that the two work hand in hand.

Unit 212 Receive and assist visitors
Element 212.2

> **You must be able to:**
> **Assist visitors**

National standard of work   **Scope**

You must always:	**You must show:**
1. Follow your organization's procedures to make sure **visitors** are comfortable while they are waiting.[1] 2. Provide **visitors** with clear directions to parts of the building they are authorized to visit.	In meeting the national standard of work you must show that you can: 1. Deal with three of the following types of **visitors**: a) internal to your organization

---

[1] For example, by offering them refreshments or directing them to a comfortable waiting area.

3. Provide **visitors** with the information they request, as long as you are able and authorized to do so.
4. If you are unable to supply information refer the visitor to someone else who can deal with their query.
5. Deal with any problems[2] politely and efficiently and in line with your organization's procedures.
6. Show empathy and determination in trying to solve any problems the visitor may have.[3]

b) external to your organization
c) expected visitors
d) unexpected visitors
e) hostile visitors

Explanations or examples of terms used:

Each organization will vary a little in terms of its precise equipment and the details considered necessary to note about each visitor. You may be able to list some of the differences between the examples below and your own situation.

---

[2] For example, the person they have come to see not expecting them or the visitor becoming angry and frustrated.

[3] For example, by showing the visitor that you understand and sympathize with their problem and that you are willing to try several approaches to solve it.

⇨ Knowledge needed to achieve standard

This section spells out the things you need to know in order to receive and assist visitors to the national standard. For some candidates many aspects of this section will seem obvious. In fact you may not even think of this information as anything special! Without it, however, you would not be able to do your job well. Other aspects you may wish to learn more about and the fact that you are taking your NVQ may provide you with the excuse to ask for some specific training.

The knowledge is sub-divided into that which covers the entire unit and that which is specific to one or other element within it.

Unit 212 Receive and assist visitors

Knowledge and understanding

You must show that you know and understand:

Unit 212 Receive and assist visitors
K1   Your organization's business and main departments.
K2   Your organization's structure and how to contact relevant departments and people.
K3   Why it is important to keep a record of visitors and who they are visiting.
K4   How to deal with hostile visitors.

Element 212.1 Receive visitors
K5   Your organization's reception procedures.
K6   The equipment and materials that you need to have and the importance of having them available and in good order.
K7   Your role in presenting a positive image of your organization and why this is important.
K8   How to greet visitors appropriately.
K9   The information you have to find out about them.
K10 Your organization's procedures for allowing entry.
K11 Details of the visit that have to be recorded.
K12 Any procedures for supplying the visitor with identification and why these are important.

Element 212.2 Assist visitors
K13 Your organization's procedures for making visitors comfortable while they are waiting.

K14 The layout of your building or site, parts which may be restricted and how to give clear directions.

K15 The range of information you are able and authorized to give, and alternative information sources.

K16 The types of problems that may occur with visitors and how to deal with these.

K17 The importance of showing visitors that you understand their problems and that you are prepared to work hard to solve them.

INTERPRETING YOUR NVQ

	Yes	No
Have you chosen one unit that matches work you regularly do?	☐	☐
Does the unit introduction (and element titles) confirm this as one of your regular activities?	☐	☐
Can you think of several specific occasions for which you can find evidence to tell the story of how you carried out this activity?	☐	☐
Have you carefully read each section of the unit relating each one to the kinds of evidence you think you might be able to collect?	☐	☐
Have you begun to relate the evidence requirements and assessment guidance to the details of performance and knowledge?	☐	☐
Have you begun to feel that the unit is merely reflecting your work and is asking for products from your work quite familiar to you?	☐	☐
If your answer to most of these questions is 'Yes' you are ready to learn about putting a portfolio together and starting to collect your evidence! (see page 80)	☐	☐

9. SPOTLIGHT ON A VERY DIFFERENT NVQ UNIT

> ⇨ Introduction to the NVQ unit
>
> ⇨ Knowledge needed to achieve standard
>
> ⇨ Essential unit knowledge
>
> ⇨ Standard to which you must work
>
> ⇨ Evidence and assessment
>
> ⇨ Key skills

This NVQ chapter is based on the National Occupational Standards for Ports developed by the industry. For further information contact: Port Skills and Safety Ltd, Africa House, 64–78 Kingsway, London WC2B 6AH. Tel: 020 7242 3538, info@portskillsandsafety.co.uk.

Note: The author's commentary is in italics.

⇨ Introduction to the NVQ unit

The scene is set in which this section or unit of an NVQ will take place. It has two sub-sections or elements. It is suited to someone whose work is controlling vehicle movements in a port.

Unit P2 Controlling vehicle movements

Unit summary

Passenger vehicles may include cars, vans, minibuses, motorhomes, and coaches. They arrive in the port either by road, or off a vessel. Safe routes for these vehicles need to be established and their movements controlled using direction signs and marshalling techniques.

This unit is in two parts. The first element covers preparation for vehicle movements, whilst the second deals with directing drivers and assisting with any unexpected situation.

An individual who meets the demands of this unit should be able to work effectively, under supervision, ensuring safe control of vehicle movements within the port.

Unit map

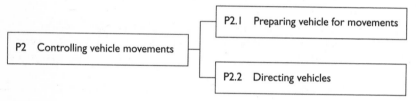

P2   Controlling vehicle movements

P2.1   Preparing vehicle for movements

P2.2   Directing vehicles

Figure 9.1

⇨ **Knowledge needed to achieve standard**

This section spells out the things you need to know in order to control vehicle movements to the national standard. For some candidates many aspects of this section will seem obvious. In fact you may not even think of this information as anything special! Without it, however, you would not be able to do your job well. Other aspects you may wish you learnt more about and the fact that you are taking your NVQ may provide you with the excuse to ask for some specific training.

The knowledge is sub-divided into that which covers the entire unit and that which is specific to one or other element within the unit. It is a good example of the inclusion of compliance mentioned in Chapter 7, p 49.

⇨ **Essential unit knowledge**

The following areas of knowledge are essential for all elements of this unit and need to be properly understood before a candidate can be considered fully competent. If any other areas of essential knowledge are required, they are included within each element.

KP6   The requirements of legislation with regard to the movement of pedestrians and vehicles and what is meant by 'safe practice'.

KP7   Identification of factors which could constitute a safety risk including hazards and obstructions to passenger movement and other port operations.

KP17   The content of emergency plans and procedures, the roles and responsibilities of those involved and the resources available for dealing with incidents.

KP24   An awareness of relevant sections legislation affecting passenger operations.

KP27   Reasons for ensuring that directions given to passengers are correct and accurate.

KP28   Ways of locating and interpreting passenger information (vessel arrival/departure times, destination information, designated locations for vehicles, vehicle segregation requirements).

KP38   Identification of vehicle destinations and interpretation of traffic signs.

KP40   Layout of the port area.

⇨ **Standard to which you must work**

Clearly listed are all the actions you must always take to work to the national standard in your duties preparing for vehicle movements. If you think about it, each of these actions is one which you would wish to be taken by someone planning for the direction of traffic in a port in which you might drive.

In this NVQ the context is integrated with the Standard.

P2.1 Preparing for vehicle movements

Element summary

This element covers the planning and preparation required to deal with vehicle movements within the port. It involves obtaining and taking account of such information as sailing times, passenger numbers, etc. Knowledge of traffic routes and movements, as well as access and signage requirements must be included in the planning.

Element knowledge

The knowledge for this element is shown at unit level and as such must all be addressed to meet this element.

Performance statements

The following standards must be achieved for a candidate to be assessed as competent at planning vehicle movements:

1. Where required by company procedures, there should be close liaison with the vessel's Loading Officer to make sure that knowledge of loading requirements is always up to date.
2. Traffic movement and build-up must be closely monitored.
3. Planning to deal with anticipated vehicle movements should be accomplished in good time, before the arrival of the vessel.
4. Information and signs needed to assist vehicles as they move through the port should be provided. Confirmation should be obtained that these resources are available at the required time and location. These resources will relate to facilities such as:

    ● ticketing

- security
- immigration
- customs
- passenger facilities

5. Information on sailing times, passenger numbers, and the vessel's berth will need to be obtained.

6. Vehicle movements must comply with company policy and statutory requirements.

7. Checks must be made on all vehicle access routes to ensure they are clear. Corrective action should be taken if necessary.

8. All direction signs should be checked to ensure that they are clearly visible and located in the correct positions.

9. The correct location for any ramp or linkspan should be checked before operations commence.

⇨ **Evidence and assessment**

Whereas the example given in the previous chapter includes evidence and guidance in some informal notes, this NVQ states both the requirements and guidance in a more formal manner. As the candidate you can see precisely how much evidence you must present and what kinds of evidence are considered particularly suitable. You might like to prepare a list of examples of types of evidence you can most easily collect in your job.

P2.1 *Preparing for vehicle movements*

Evidence requirements

The candidate must demonstrate that he/she consistently meets the required standards when **planning vehicle movements**. The evidence must include:

- A minimum of two observations of the candidate preparing to direct traffic movement. These observations must confirm that all of the necessary checks have been carried out prior to operations commencing.
- A record of responses made to questions put to the candidate in relation to the above observations.
- Demonstration of competence in a variety of circumstances i.e. in at least three of the categories of passenger facility identified in Performance Statement 4.
- Where the port has a limited number of these facilities (ie less than three), the candidate must demonstrate his or her competence with regard to all of those facilities that are present.

Assessment guidance

The following are examples of evidence that would be acceptable for this element:

- Testimonies from other members of staff, confirming conversations that the candidate has participated in and checks that he or she has carried out.
- Records of information obtained by the candidate that impacts on specific traffic movements e.g. vessel sailing times, vessel berthing arrangements.
- Responses to questions on aspects of procedure and safety.

Candidate notes

Element completed:

Candidate's signature:

⇨ **Standard to which you must work**

Clearly listed are all the actions you must always take to work to the national standard in your duties directing vehicles in a port. If you think about it, each of these actions is one which you would wish to be taken by someone directing you when you are driving in a port.

In this NVQ the context is integrated with the Standard.

P2.2 Directing vehicles

Element summary

Safe and efficient passage through the port to their next destination. This may be the checking-in facility, information desk, customs, security, road links, etc. Individuals need to be constantly on the alert for drivers who require information or directions and should be prepared to offer assistance.

Element knowledge

The following areas of knowledge are essential and need to be properly understood before an individual can be considered fully competent in this operation.

KP37   Procedures and techniques for communicating using hand signals.

KP39   Compliance with traffic management measures.

KP46   Basic vehicle maintenance techniques.

KP47   Responses to traffic hold-ups and congestion.

Performance statements

The following standards must be achieved for a candidate to be assessed as competent at directing vehicles:

1.   Drivers arriving in the port should be directed to the correct location. Their vehicles should be correctly positioned and segregated in preparation for loading operations.

2.   The safety of passengers, self and other port operatives must be considered when directing vehicles. Safety measures will include:
   ● wearing visible protective clothing and steel toe-caps
   ● complying with safety legislation

3.   Any hand signals used to direct vehicle movements must be clear and easily understood by vehicle drivers.

4.   Traffic movements must be controlled in such a way that a smooth traffic flow is maintained at all times.

5.   Enquiries from drivers and passengers should be handled

in a courteous and helpful manner and in a way that avoids delay to other vehicles.

6. Requests for traffic management measures to be put into place should be responded to speedily.

7. Any unexpected situations should be dealt with quickly and effectively. These may include:
   - vehicle breakdowns
   - congestion

8. Any drivers found to be having difficulties should be approached. If the problem can be solved, this should be achieved as quickly as possible. Where this is not possible, further assistance should be sought from vehicle assistance services.

⇨ Evidence and assessment

Whereas the example given in the previous chapter includes evidence and guidance in some informal notes, this NVQ states both the requirements and guidance in a more formal manner. As the candidate you can see precisely how much evidence you must present and what kinds of evidence are considered particularly suitable. You might like to prepare a list of examples of types of evidence you can most easily collect in your job.

P2.2 Directing vehicles

Evidence requirements

The candidate must demonstrate that he/she consistently meets the required standards when directing vehicles. The evidence must include:

- A minimum of three observations of the candidate directing vehicles within the port area. Where possible, each observation should take place in a different location and under different weather conditions. One observation must take place at a time when traffic flow is high and when vehicle delays are being experienced.
- Separately to the above, at least four observations of the candidate responding to others. Two observations should involve responding to queries from drivers and/or passengers and two should involve responding to information provided by colleagues or other port staff.
- A record of responses made to questions put to the candidate in relation to the above observations.

Assessment guidance

The following are examples of evidence that would be acceptable for this element:

- Responses the candidate has made to questions on aspects of procedure and safety.
- A log the candidate has compiled of queries and comments made by drivers, and details of any responses which he or she has given and any action that was taken as a consequence.

● Demonstration of
competence in both of the
circumstances identified in
Performance Statement 7.

Candidate notes

Element completed:

Candidate's signature:

⇨ **Key Skills**

There is a discussion of Key Skills in the next chapter. This is an excellent example of Key Skills seen as an essential part of an NVQ. Sections from the range of Key Skills have been selected without which it cannot accept that the job is being done to the national standard. The unit is not complete without these.

Key Skills

The activities required to be undertaken in this NVQ unit may also provide an opportunity to generate evidence for the following Key (Core) Skills:

- Communication – Take part in discussions (Level 2)
- Communication – Read and respond to written materials (Level 1)
- Working with Others – Identify collective goals and responsibilities (Level 1)
- Working with Others – Work to collective goals (Level 1)

In some instances, the **same** evidence may be relevant to both the NVQ and the Key (Core) Skills. In other instances, it may be necessary to collect **additional** evidence for the Key (Core) Skills.

Unit completed

Date: _____

Candidate's signature: _____

Note: The above signature confirms that the unit has been completed. Candidates will also be required to complete their Assessment Record log.

Don't forget

- Relate the different sections of the NVQ unit to each other.

- Read each sentence carefully – it's all there to help you.

- Make sure you demonstrate how you work to the standard *and* how you do so in any circumstances.

- Show that you can use all relevant equipment competently *and* that you have the required knowledge to support what you do.

10. THE WIDER WORLD OF NVQs

⇨ How NVQs started

⇨ A development from NVQs

⇨ Key Skills

⇨ Technical Certificate

⇨ Modern Apprenticeships

⇨ The future for NVQs?

⇨ How NVQs started

When NVQs were first developed they were based on occupational standards of best current practice drawn up by each sector of work.

Occupational standards > NVQs

⇨ **A development from NVQs**

To improve the quality of training and skills for young people, the Modern Apprenticeship was created based on NVQs. The Modern Apprenticeship provides a training package in which an NVQ is central and Key Skills are also included.

NVQs > Modern Apprenticeships

Modern Apprenticeships are available at two levels. These are Foundation Modern Apprenticeship (FMA) and Advanced Modern Apprenticeship (AMA). The FMA will include an NVQ at Level 2 or above and will normally require 18 months to two years.The AMA will include at least a Level 3 NVQ and will usually extend over two or three years.

MODERN APPRENTICESHIP (MA)

Foundation Level (FMA)
Includes:

- NVQ Level 2+
- Usually takes 18 months to two years

Advanced Level (AMA)
Includes:

- NVQ Level 3+
- Usually takes two to three years

Modern Apprenticeships are available in 70 sectors varying from Business Administration to Hairdresssing, Engineering, Estate Agency and the Motor Industry.

⇨ **Key Skills**

These are the kinds of skill that people need to do any job satisfactorily and in their non-working lives. There are three main Key Skills:

- Communication
- Application of number
- Information technology

And three wider Key Skills:

- Working with others
- Problem solving
- Improving own learning and performance

Key Skills are available individually at Levels 1–4 and as a single integrated package called Personal Skills Development at Level 5. Mostly the levels of Key Skills are specified for each Modern Apprenticeship, however, Level 2 in Communication and Application of Number are a requirement for all Advanced Modern Apprenticeships.

KEY SKILLS

- Levels 1–4
- Personal Skills Development Level 5

All Advanced Modern Apprenticeships include at least

- Level 2 Communication and Application of Number

Although there is no minimum Key Skills requirement for Foundation Modern Apprenticeships, trainees are encouraged to undertake Key Skills at the appropriate level to their needs and abilities.

You develop a portfolio for Key Skills in just the same way as you do for an NVQ. In fact it is very likely that you will be able to re-use – by cross-referencing – evidence from your NVQ portfolio in support of your Key Skills.

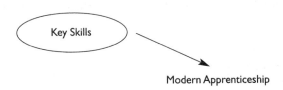

Modern Apprenticeship

⇨ Technical Certificate

Like Key Skills, the Technical Certificate was developed as a discrete part of the Modern Apprenticeship. The Knowledge within an NVQ has been separated from the rest to make the learning and assessment more convenient.

The Modern Apprentice is assessed as far as possible on the job for the practical skills s/he has acquired and in all probability off the job for the knowledge which supports those practical skills. Sometimes the qualification will be entirely new and sometimes it will be an existing qualification which is directly linked with the UK occupational standards from which NVQs are developed.

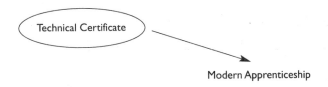

Modern Apprenticeship

⇨ **Modern Apprenticeships**

As we have seen above, Modern Apprenticeships are NVQs and more. With the NVQ at their heart they also include Key Skills and a Technical Certificate along with a commitment from an employer to provide a job with the necessary experience. Local Learning Skills Councils may provide financial support and funding is normally available for 16, 17 and 18 year olds. This will often be through a training provider. For details of your Learning Skills Council, check the Web site listed at the back of this book.

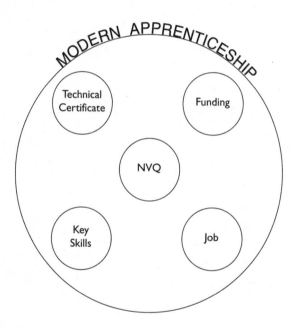

⇨ **The future for NVQs?**

The work on monitoring and improving NVQs is set to continue. In the future they will also relate more closely to the qualifications used in other countries. It is expected that they will be much more commonly used than now as the basis for job profiles, for recruiting new staff and for the planning which all kinds of staff organizations will continue to need for internal appraisals and for training and development.

It was always foreseen that NVQs could be used in these ways, as the chapter *Persuading your boss about NVQs* suggests. However, it is now the intention that these uses be encouraged and promoted more strongly than in the past.

You may hear talk of *business analysis* where you work. This too can be founded upon the work done to prepare NVQs. The outcomes of your work as stated in the NVQ for which you are preparing can provide the analysis of the functions you perform. Imagine adding these outcomes right across an organization. You would get a good picture of the business activities. The more practical way to approach this is from the picture of the outcomes of the entire sector, scaled down to the outcomes of your organization. In fact it was from this picture for your whole sector of work that your occupational standards were first drawn up.

THE FUTURE

● Quality improving all the time

Additional uses:

● job profiles
● recruitment
● staff planning
● internal appraisal
● training and development
And for business analysis

WORTH LOOKING INTO

Modern Apprenticeships (MAs)

- Foundation (FMAs)

- Advanced (AMAs)

Key Skills

Technical Certificates

Ask at your nearest Learning Skills Council!

11. A PORTFOLIO?

⇨ Work project, not school project

⇨ Contents

⇨ Career history

⇨ Context of assessment

⇨ Assessment forms

⇨ Evidence

⇨ Arrangement of portfolio

⇨ Useful after assessment

All you need to start work on your portfolio are: a ring binder, dividers, a hole punch, a glue stick, clear plastic pockets, plain white and coloured paper, coloured labels and coloured pens.

⇨ **Work project, not school project**

If you have children of school age or if you are of the generation that has done a good deal of project work during your own school education, you will quickly take to the portfolio. It is literally the work version of a school project! Just like a school project, a portfolio is a convenient way of arranging a great variety of material. The successful portfolio shows that you have really got under the skin of the area about which you have been learning.

If you are not familiar with school projects, the portfolio concept may be a little harder to grasp. Art students will take a selection of their work in a portfolio to an interview, whether for a place at college or for a job, to prove their standard and range of ability. This is largely because a few sentences on a piece of paper or a single examination grade are quite insufficient as a means of demonstrating practical ability. Your portfolio as an NVQ candidate will also be used as proof of how well you carry out your work.

However, the NVQ portfolio is not a random selection so much as a concise collection of evidence of your ability to carry out the requirements of a specific unit, or group of units, towards an NVQ. Most often, like the school project, it will be held in a ring binder. However, some bulky items, such as videos, may not fit into it but this does not matter. You will simply find another container.

PORTFOLIO

- Consists of a variety of material
- Comprises a concise collection
- Is like an artist's portfolio
- Is proof of ability and understanding
- Is usually contained in a ring binder

⇨ **Contents**

First you will need a title page, as in any book, which will give your own details and those of the NVQ unit to which the portfolio refers. Next comes a contents list. This should itemize the main headings but not every scrap of information within the binder. The list will follow the order of arrangement within the binder and lead the assessor to the page number or the section where the particular area of information starts.

Like everything else within your portfolio, the contents list is included to make it easier for your assessor to find his or her way through your evidence. The contents list is a major signpost.

PORTFOLIO CONTENTS LIST

- Is a signpost
- Includes main headings
- Is in order of arrangement
- Is easy for the reader to follow

⇨ **Career history**

It is not essential to include in your portfolio an outline of your career (curriculum vitae). However, particularly if your assessor does not already know you very well, this could provide a much more rounded picture of you and your working life. It may save you answering some queries yourself. More importantly, if you are largely being assessed on the basis of your portfolio but are not necessarily sitting there while it is being studied, it will give the assessor the chance to get to know you in your absence.

You may already have a curriculum vitae (CV) prepared. Check it, and update it if necessary. If you do not already have one, prepare a simple list of the jobs you have done, and include your job title, the name of the organization for which you were working, and the dates you worked there. When the job seems particularly relevant to the NVQ you are taking, be sure to include details of your main duties and experience of value in the NVQ. Details of relevant qualifications you have already taken should be included as these may help you to prove your Underpinning Knowledge and Understanding. A CV can be lengthy and complicated. However, for this purpose it should be brief and straightforward. You might like to attach a photo of yourself – again, it can help your assessor.

CAREER HISTORY

- Rounded picture of you
- Up to date
- Relevant jobs and achievements listed
- Relevant main duties outlined
- Relevant qualifications listed
- Brief and straightforward

⇨ Context of assessment

This section is an opportunity for you to write one or two paragraphs describing the background to your current job situation in which you are being assessed for your NVQ. Describe, insofar as it is relevant, the organization in which you are being assessed. You may wish to include an organization chart showing your own position as well as outlining the type and size of organization. Your job description would be useful here. If there are regular witness statements from the same people included in your portfolio, it would be helpful to give some information to put them in context.

If your assessor is your line manager it may seem odd to explain what you do and where and why you do it – after all, your line manager should know! However, the internal verifier, who may be further away from you within the organization, may not know much about what you do. The internal verifier oversees the assessor. For the candidate who is registered at an assessment centre outside the place of work it will be vital to explain the context in which the evidence has been collected. The external verifier, who comes to the assessment centre on behalf of the awarding body, will also need this background information. The external verifier oversees and advises the assessment centre.

Consider what you write on context to be your opportunity to point out anything that may need explaining. Perhaps some jobs are done seasonally and others occur very rarely. Possibly you have a special skill or unusual experience.

CONTEXT INCLUDES:

- The organization in which you gathered your evidence
- Where you fit in the organization
- Background to witnesses who have provided assessment evidence for your portfolio
- What you do and why you do it

and the context should make the portfolio easier for the reader to understand

---

⇨ Assessment forms

Awarding bodies and individual assessment centres may vary in the number and arrangement of their assessment forms. At the least you must expect to complete a form for each element and often another one summarizing each unit. Your assessor will make sure that you understand how to do this. For your own purposes you may prepare additional forms yourself to standardize the format in which you provide certain types of evidence, for example, witness reports.

Just like the contents list, these forms should be viewed as signposts.

The unit form is likely to appear the least complicated and will provide an overview. There may be other grids and checklists for confirming the detailed evidence and knowledge. These should be cross-referenced to your portfolio and each item given a unique reference number.

At first glance this form may appear slightly daunting. If you think of it as the main link with your collection of evidence, then it should begin to make sense. There are so many strands involved that it has to have a good many columns. This is the point at which the assessor is able to cross-check that everything has been covered. These forms are the links holding the portfolio together.

ASSESSMENT FORMS

- Provide signposts through the evidence
- May be expected at least for units
- Act as the main links in a portfolio
- Contain a unique reference number for each item of evidence

⇨ Evidence

Your evidence should tell the story of your working life. Take one unit. Look at the unit title and, where there is one, the introduction to the unit. Then gather the items in which you capably perform its activity on say, two or three occasions. Next, look at the detail within the unit (and its elements). You will probably find that the items you have gathered, between them, cover most of the detail. For example, every time you handle a complaint from a tricky customer you will call upon different facets of your communication skills.

Usually several units of your NVQ will lend themselves to being approached at the same time. Their activities will overlap. Once you have gathered the main story of each of this group of units you should cross-reference that evidence to the detail within the units. Most of the gaps will be filled from evidence you first gathered for an overlapping unit. Only now is it time to look further afield for evidence beyond the main stories you have told.

You should select your evidence economically for its value as proof of your competence in a particular aspect of an element. It is only useful if it is specific. In Chapter 6 it was explained that evidence for your assessment may be written, oral or visual. You will have no trouble placing sheets of written information or photographs in your ring binder portfolio. More difficult may be the video, cassette or large plan. There is no problem with any of these formats provided they contain valuable evidence.

You will need to be a little more imaginative in finding a means of storage and arrangement for bulkier kinds of evidence. If they are held in a separate container, this must be indicated on the element form. Each item of evidence will be identified on the element form by its unique reference number.

Evidence should be dated and, if it is from a team exercise (perhaps a report of a meeting in which you took part), the extent of your contribution needs to be confirmed. Your evidence should show that you are currently competent. This means that if you are including Accreditation of Prior Learning (APL) in your portfolio, this prior skill must be shown still to be relevant. APL means the formal acknowledgement of evidence of skills you already possess. These skills must be to the level of the current national standard.

EVIDENCE SHOULD BE:

- The story of your work
- Economical
- Well stored
- Uniquely referenced by number
- Current
- Still relevant if APL
- Confirmed if teamwork

⇨ **Arrangement of portfolio**

Your goal in choosing how to arrange your portfolio is to make it easy for your assessor to find things. Several alternative arrangements will probably occur to you as you are gathering your work together. Provided that goal is foremost in your mind, it does not matter which means you choose. At the outset, however, you should explain your method of arrangement and also provide a key to abbreviations and jargon. If you are certain these terms are used throughout your occupation your assessor and verifiers should be fully conversant with them. However, some jargon and abbreviations will be used within your organization only and the external verifier cannot be expected to understand these – no more can your assessor if you are using an assessment centre outside your workplace.

You might decide to file all the evidence relating to one unit behind its form. If so do not forget when a piece of evidence relates to more than one unit (a letter, memo or report will often refer to more than one activity) that although it can only be filed in one place, your cross-referencing should make it easy to find from other points in the portfolio.

Alternatively you may decide that the easiest method of arrangement is by type of evidence. You place all records of telephone calls together, all photographs together, all memos, budgets, reports of meetings, and so on in separate sections. Once again with clear cross-referencing it should be straightforward to link back from the element form.

If you want a slim portfolio which uses your evidence economically, try a single, numbered sequence of evidence for the entire NVQ. You file all introductory sections to the portfolio and the forms at the front. Next file the evidence and number it from 1 to infinity. Simple numbers, without decimal points or letters of the alphabet attached, are all that you need. No particular order is necessary. The only sign-post necessary is the cross-referencing on your element form! Candidates using this particular arrangement seem more inclined to apply individual items of evidence to many elements and units. If you choose this method you should be able to carry your own portfolio – without the help of a supermarket trolley!

Colour will not only brighten up your portfolio but will also provide an additional means of leading your assessor through it. A particular colour might indicate the format of the evidence or it might be chosen to represent a specific element so that everything relating to it is marked with that colour. Like all other signposting, colour coding can be invaluable provided that it is logical, clear and consistent.

Have a look in a good stationers and buy a range of materials to help you to make your portfolio easy to follow and so attractive to look at that you feel it is an achievement in itself, of which you may be justifiably proud.

One word of warning – do not make your portfolio over-complicated!

Arrangement of portfolio should be:

- Made easy for assessor
- Explained: arrangement, referencing, abbreviations, jargon
- Arranged logically
- Colour coded
- Not over-complicated

⇨ Useful after assessment

Some organizations will be introducing NVQs as part of a new approach to personnel and training based entirely upon the occupational standards. In these organizations you will expect to take your current portfolio to performance reviews and appraisals. It will provide a focus for discussion.

If, however, you work for an organization that is not itself an assessment centre, your line manager may not be familiar with NVQ portfolios. It might be something to take along and offer to be looked at in the appraisal. If your work does not normally include the arrangement of documents, writing or photography – all of which skills have been necessary to build up the portfolio – this will be a way of drawing to your boss's attention these previously hidden abilities. Your work too is likely to gain renewed respect when well presented on paper. It is very easy for others to forget just how many components there are to your job.

Similarly, your portfolio is something to take with you to an interview for a prospective new job. Again, it will provide a focus, and while you will not expect the interviewer to read it page by page, your portfolio should give an impression you are a well-organized person able to present yourself and your ideas well. You should know your own way round your portfolio so that you can quickly turn up an item in support of a point you are making in conversation.

A good portfolio will take time and trouble to prepare. Make it work for you!

After assessment the portfolio:

- May be used at appraisal
- Shows additional organizational skills
- Provides status for work
- May be used at interviews

SHOPPING LIST
FOR
PORTFOLIO STARTER KIT

Ring binder
Dividers
Hole punch
Glue stick
Clear plastic pockets
Plain white paper
Plain coloured paper
Coloured pens
Coloured labels

This list will start you off but as time goes on you will devise your own way of designing your portfolio.

12. WHAT NEXT?

⇨ Certificate for unit

⇨ Build units into NVQ

or

⇨ Select units from different sectors

⇨ Certificate for unit

You do not have to set aside years of your life to work for an NVQ. Every time you are assessed as competent in all the elements that make up a unit, you will be certificated. You should consider this unit as a mini qualification in its own right, awarded for the particular skill in which you have been assessed. On its own a unit certificate is something to prove your ability if, for instance, you are applying for a promotion or a new job.

⇨ Build units into NVQ

Most candidates will probably be aiming for a whole NVQ. Depending on the level of NVQ – and therefore the complexity and difficulty of the work – the number of units, or elements within each unit, may increase.

At the end of building up the necessary number of units you will be assessed in your work as competent to a particular level. This assessment is likely to provide you and your job with a status. You should find it easier to gauge your own level and that of your job in relation to others, particularly in relation to promotions or job moves.

Some NVQs will be made up of the parts described in the diagram below. Others will seem less complicated as they will only contain some of these parts. Don't let this worry you. All are equally valid NVQs – regardless of style – that have been accredited by the QCA.

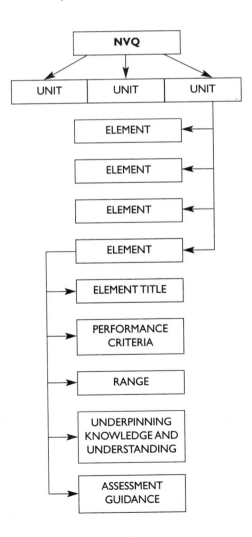

⇨ **Select units from different sectors**

Some jobs just do not fit tidily into an exact NVQ. While the aim in · devising the system has been to reflect the real job situation, a national system could not hope to encompass every single job in existence.

Think of a post advertised as Secretary/Information Assistant, for example. It is very likely that such a job would in part be reflected by an Administration NVQ (these cover standard secretarial posts) and additionally, because there is a clear emphasis on information, some units from an Information and Library Services NVQ. It sounds as if the holder of a job like this will find the information-handling unit from Administration insufficiently detailed. On the other hand, taking a complete Information and Library Services NVQ would exaggerate the information component of the job.

Other jobs people hold will have an even greater mix of activities within them. If yours is one of these I expect it will be reflected in a selection of units from an assortment of occupations. On the other hand you may prefer to try to get the necessary experience to gain a whole NVQ in the area of work most emphasized within your job. The choice has to be yours.

However, a mixed bag of units from different work areas will demonstrate your skills but will not make it easy for a future employer to gauge the level at which you operate. Units do not have levels. Only whole NVQs are assigned to levels (see page 95 for more about levels).

There is also the likelihood that the selection of units that so well reflects your current job may be so specialized as to reflect no other job in existence! If you think this may be the case, seek advice from the assessment centre at which you were thinking of registering. The staff there will be able to advise you how to maximize the benefits of NVQ units from the point of view of your own career.

PROGRESS LIST

This progress list is here to remind you what you will learn about NVQs in this book and what stage you have reached so far.

☑ What is an NVQ?

☑ Why take an NVQ?

☑ How to become an NVQ candidate

☑ What is an assessment centre?

☑ What does the assessor do?

☑ What do candidates do?

☑ How to find your way around an NVQ

☑ Focus on an NVQ unit

☑ Spotlight on a very different NVQ unit

☑ The wider world of NVQs

☑ A portfolio?

☑ What next?

☐ The NVQ framework

☐ Persuading your boss about NVQs

13. THE NVQ FRAMEWORK

⇨ More like a climbing frame

⇨ Upward progression

⇨ Sideways progression

⇨ Comparable and transferable skills

⇨ More like a climbing frame

With what should the flexible NVQ system be compared? It is not like a snakes and ladders board because, unlike the traditional qualifications systems in which examination failure is not uncommon, there are no snakes to fall down!

Nor is it a ladder. Some candidates may well choose to progress upwards and achieve higher and higher levels of certification in their chosen field. Others may prefer breadth to height, and progress sideways, broadening their skills base.

Many candidates, like children on a climbing frame, will sometimes move up and sometimes across. This will be true when a candidate is seeking to show an ability to transfer between job types.

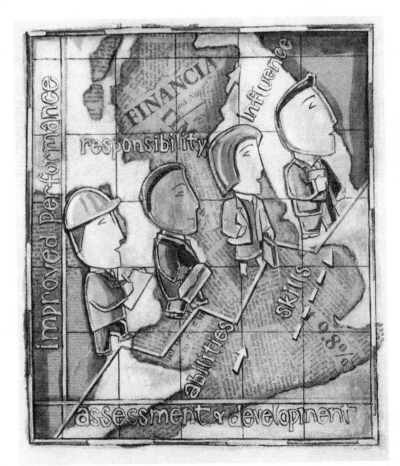

© MCI

⇨ Upward progression

There are five levels of NVQ. Not all have been developed in every occupation and indeed some levels will never be prepared for some occupations.

The NVQ ladder may be joined at any rung which seems the appropriate point for you. It is not always necessary to work through from Level 1 to Level 5.

The definitions below describing NVQ levels are the official ones laid down by the former National Council for Vocational Qualifications (predecessor of QCA the Qualifications and Curriculum Authority). They come from NVQ Criteria and Guidance, published by NCVQ in 1995. Like much 'Civil Service speak' they are not an example of clarity. Your assessor should be able to tell you how they apply to you. I have added some headings in italic as a quick guide to what the different levels mean, however, these may vary slightly from one sector to another.

Routine work
Level 1: competence which involves the application of knowledge in the performance or a range of varied work activities, most of which may be routine or predictable.

Some varied work with responsibility
Level 2: competence which involves the application of knowledge in a significant range of varied work activities, performed in a variety of contexts. Some of the activities are complex or non-routine, and there is some individual responsibility or autonomy. Collaboration with others, perhaps through membership of a work group or team, may often be a requirement.

Some supervision of others
Level 3: competence which involves the application of knowledge in a broad range of varied work activities performed in a wide variety of contexts, most of which are complex and non-routine. There is considerable responsibility and autonomy, and control or guidance of others is often required.

Junior professional work/junior management
Level 4: competence which involves the application of knowledge in a broad range of complex, technical or professional work activities performed in a wide variety of contexts and with a substantial degree of personal responsibility and autonomy. Responsibility for the work of others and the allocation of resources is often present.

Experienced professional work/management
Level 5: competence which involves the application of a significant range of fundamental principles across a wide and often unpredictable variety of contexts. Very substantial personal autonomy and often significant responsibility for the work of others and for the allocation of substantial resources feature strongly, as do personal accountabilities for analysis and diagnosis, design, planning, execution and evaluation.

REASONS FOR SIDEWAYS PROGRESSION

- Career change
- Occupation demands new skills:
    computing
    commercial skill

⇨ Sideways progression

Nowadays many of us will change the course of our careers several times. Some skills become redundant and the market grows for others.

As organizations and jobs within them develop, so staff have to acquire new and often very different skills. A good example of this is how since the mid-1970s increasing numbers of people have had to acquire computer skills.

Similarly, since about 1980 many people working in previously 'free to the customer' services have had their roles widened to encompass a commercial side. Examples of this can be found in education, librarianship and museum work.

⇨ Comparable and transferable skills

The whole NVQ framework (below) shows that there are 11 broad areas of competence. Within each of these areas are five levels of achievement. There are 124 sets of qualifications available now, or ready soon (a list is provided on pages 117–18). As it is possible to move between areas of competence, up and down levels of achievement, the possible scope is enormous.

The 11 areas of competence in the NVQ framework are:

Tending animals, plants and land

Extracting and providing natural resources

Constructing

Engineering

Manufacturing

Transporting

Providing goods and services

Providing health, social care and protective services

Providing business services

Communicating

Developing and extending knowledge and skill

A huge effort has been made to keep the rules of assessment standard between all areas of competence. The aim has been to arrive at a system in which the amount of skill required for a Level 2 in Racehorse Care is exactly comparable with the skill required for a Level 2 qualification in Customer Care (through a Customer Service NVQ).

Not all the efforts have been successful, but the effort has been made. This means that holders of Level 2 qualifications in closely similar areas of competence – for instance hotel reception and retail – might be expected to transfer their jobs without much difficulty.

Also, some skills – like data handling, which comes into Administration at Level 2 – are obviously transferable across a large number of areas of competence. Once you have been assessed as competent in one of these units, you do not need to be reassessed in it, even if it appears in another NVQ which you decide to take.

SUMMARY OF THE NVQ FRAMEWORK

- Five levels
- 11 areas of competence
- 120+ groups of qualifications under development
- All levels of skill are comparable
- Some skills are transferable

SELF-ASSESSMENT

Start to work out where you fit in the framework!

You can choose between five levels of difficulty:

❑ Level 1

❑ Level 2

❑ Level 3

❑ Level 4

❑ Level 5

and between 11 areas of competence:

❑ Tending animals, plants and land

❑ Extracting and providing natural resources

❑ Constructing

❑ Engineering

❑ Manufacturing

❑ Transporting

❑ Providing goods and services

❑ Providing health, social care and protective services

❑ Providing business services

❑ Communicating

❑ Developing and extending knowledge and skill

and within the areas of competence about 120 groups of qualifications. These are listed on pages 117–18. Start to find out about the ones that interest you.

14. PERSUADING YOUR BOSS ABOUT NVQs

⇨ Higher quality output

⇨ Better motivated staff

⇨ Staff training programme towards national qualifications

⇨ Senior staff freed for new work as they can delegate more

⇨ NVQs provide structure for many personnel and training functions

⇨ Plan strategy

⇨ Obtain guidance

⇨ Plan how to fill training gaps

⇨ **Higher quality output**

Wherever you work it's a certainty that your boss will be looking for more and better outputs from the organization as a whole. The changes taking place at the moment, both in terms of customer expectations and the technology to meet the requirements are phenomenal. Changes in your work style for both these reasons will be continuous, and to manage these your learning will need to be continuous and to high current standards.

Tell your boss that staff who are qualified with NVQs will not only have practical competence, but they will also be competent as regards their knowledge of any statutory or legal obligations, health and safety requirements, critical aspects of the working environment, as well as relevant ethical, creative or value-based characteristics of the work.

NVQs have been developed to meet these needs. The time for burying heads in the sand is over – unless they are going to remain in the sand for ever!

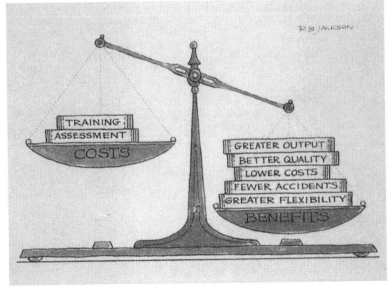

© BCCCA and Barry Jackson

NVQs WILL ASSIST HIGHER QUALITY OUTPUT

- More and better outputs expected
- Changes in customer expectations
- Changes in technology
- Changes in work style needed
- Continous learning to high standards needed

⇨ **Better motivated staff**

The stimulus of following a well-planned programme of training is bound to revive your interest in your work. Assistance to keep up with what is new and the opportunity to extend your abilities and skills are likely to make you more enthusiastic about the organization making this training available to you. This in turn makes you a more valuable employee.

NVQs RESULT IN BETTER MOTIVATED STAFF

- Well-planned training programme
- Staff's abilities maintained and extended
- Staff more enthusiastic
- Employees become more valuable

⇨ Staff training programme towards national qualifications

Training is all very well, but training leading to a national qualification is something staff can keep as their own. Job applicants will be able to prove the training they have undergone which will be helpful for both the employer and employee. This will make it easier for employees to move around and therefore easier, too, for employers to find new staff. Obtaining a national qualification as a result of training will add credibility to the training itself, and make it more highly valued by staff.

TRAINING TOWARDS A NATIONAL QUALIFICATION

- Job applicants will have proof of skills
- Staff become more mobile
- New staff easier to find
- Staff value training more

⇨ Senior staff freed for new work as they can delegate more

As staff at lower levels are trained to carry out more complex work, and technology takes over a great deal that is routine, so the more senior staff in your organization will be able to delegate more of their own work. This in turn will release those senior staff to carry out new functions, look harder for new markets, and so on. The overall effect of NVQs is to increase the skills of the entire workforce and enable more to share responsibility.

SENIOR STAFF CAN DELEGATE MORE

- Technology carries out much of routine work
- Lower levels trained to carry out more complex work
- Senior staff freed for new functions and to seek new markets
- Entire workforce increases skills

⇨ **NVQs provide structure for many personnel and training functions**

Personnel and training departments of organizations looking at NVQs for the first time should consider them as a new structure on which to hang many of their human resource management functions. The standards developed in the process of creating NVQs are an excellent management tool in their own right. They provide an immediate basis for carrying out a training needs analysis and from this may be devised your organization's whole training policy.

A great deal of time is spent writing what are often not very clear job descriptions. Once again, much of this work may be reduced by using the occupational standards as the basis.

Recruitment procedures will be a good deal more streamlined when the skills required may be explained in terms of NVQs, and skills offered by applicants explained as NVQ attainment will be immediately clear to employers.

Once in a job there is the regular appraisal routine – all too often a situation which no one knows how to handle properly. NVQs will provide a focal point for these reviews. How do an employee's skills measure up to those specified as necessary for the job? Is the assessment plan on target? For those who find the appraisal process difficult there is a new point upon which it may focus – the portfolio. Instead of awkward attempts at relaxed conversation, how about looking through the NVQ portfolio, so bringing the reality of the job into the appraisal interview?

NVQ standard as a management tool for:

- Training needs analysis
- Improved job descriptions
- Streamlined recruitment procedures
- Point of focus for appraisals

⇨ **Plan strategy**

If you are trying to persuade your boss that your organization should become an assessment centre for NVQs you will need to understand the process yourself. It will take the most determined organization some time if it is starting from scratch – so don't expect to start on your NVQ next week if your organization is not yet an assessment centre!

If you work for a large organization it may already be approved as an assessment centre for some NVQs but not for others. If it is not approved for the one you and your colleagues want to take but the same awarding body offers it, the process will be a lot quicker.

If there are only a few people in your organization who are likely to take the NVQ you want, your boss might do better to assist you to use a centre elsewhere, such as a college or an independent training organization.

Many organizations contain small specialist departments servicing their main business. Major retail groups have selling as their main activity. Approval for assessment for selling makes sense. It is likely that such a group would also wish to assess buying, administration and management. However, it might not have enough potential candidates to make accounting, design or information and library services viable for in-house assessment. For such candidates it might be more sensible to purchase the services of other providers. Another option would be to join a consortium assessment centre. (See Chapter 4 on the different types of centre available.)

No matter which course your boss decides to follow, it will still be necessary to plan a careful strategy.

- What does the organization expect to gain from NVQs?
- How many staff are likely to take an NVQ?
- Will an experimental trial be run before the whole organization starts to use NVQs?
- Will the trial use staff from one department or a member of staff from every department?
- Over how long a period will the pilot run?
- Will it rely on volunteers?
- How will its value to the organization be assessed?
- Who will take the lead?
- What support will be given to candidates?
- What are the resourcing implications?

A glance at this list, which is by no means exhaustive, will make you realize that a good deal is involved.

PLAN STRATEGY

- Allow time
- Find out whether already centre for some NVQs
- Consider numbers of candidates
- Consider use of another centre
- Consider membership of consortium
- Find means of gauging organizational gains
- Consider NVQ trial first
- Provide support to candidates
- Obtain resourcing

⇨ Obtain guidance

Your employer, like you, will have a number of different organizations to turn to for advice. The Qualifications and Curriculum Authority (QCA) or the local Learning and Skills Council (LSC) will be able to supply general information such as which NVQs are available, which standards setting body developed them and which awarding bodies offer them. The LSC is likely to be able to provide information on other organizations in the same area offering the NVQ your organization is contemplating. Detailed information will be available from the appropriate standards-setting body and awarding body. NVQs which cover the work of a large part of the working population are frequently offered by several awarding bodies.

Your employer will be able to receive details of coverage of the NVQ, the direct costs and application forms from the awarding body. It is the expert organization in all aspects concerning administration and assessment of the NVQ. The standards-setting body, which represents the work area, may be able to give practical guidance based on the experience of how others have done it. Both should be actively trying to encourage take-up.

The awarding body, for a modest fee, will often be able to offer a single advisory visit to a prospective centre. Some organizations, however, without the spare staff to put into planning for NVQs and with no previous experience, may prefer to obtain consultancy help through the planning and introductory period.

Your organization can obtain guidance from:

- QCA
- the local Learning and Skills Council
- the appropriate standards setting body
- the awarding body for the particular NVQ

⇨ Plan how to fill training gaps

You will no doubt be persuading your boss that NVQs are less disruptive to work flow – and more relevant to the workplace – than traditional day-release courses. However, there is no point in trying to hide the fact that to achieve NVQs, training will undoubtedly be necessary.

Whether the training is carried out by your line manager at the same time as doing the job, whether computer-assisted learning facilities or video training are supplied at work, whether trainers are brought in or you are sent out for training, it will still cost both time and money. The idea behind the NVQ movement is to improve the skills of the working population and so make it produce to higher levels of quality and efficiency. You don't do this by only giving out certificates. To be entitled to the certificates, staff must work to national standards and it is in the interests of their employers to help staff to achieve these.

Final word

You may by now be thinking, 'This sounds great from my boss's point of view but how about me?' Well, the whole point is that NVQs will be good for you both.

You now know how to get an NVQ and how to introduce your organization to the idea of becoming part of the NVQ world. Early on in this book you read that NVQs are about doing. So have a look at the last three reference sections and then go out and do. *Go and get yourself registered for an NVQ!*

WHERE TO FIND OUT MORE

Regulatory bodies

Qualifications and Curriculum Authority (QCA)
82 Piccadilly, London, W1J 8QA
Tel. 020 7509 5555; Fax. 020 7509 6666
e-mail *info@qca.org.uk*
WWW *http://www.open.gov.uk/qca/*

QCA Northern Ireland
2nd floor, Glendinning House
6 Murray Street, Belfast, BT1 6DN
Tel. 028 90330706; Fax. 028 90231621
e-mail *infoni@qca.org.uk*
WWW *http://www.open.gov.uk/qca/*

Qualifications, Curriculum and Assessment Authority for Wales (ACCAC)
Castle Building, Womanby Street, Cardiff, CF10 1SX
Tel. 0292037 5400; Fax. 09920 229642
e-mail *info@accac.org.uk*
WWW *http://www.accac.org.uk*

Scottish Qualifications Authority (SQA)
Hanover House
24 Douglas Street, Glasgow, G2 7NQ
Tel. 0845 279 1000; Fax. 0141 242 2244
e-mail *helpdesk@sqa.org.uk*
WWW *http://www.sqa.org.uk*

Overseas enquiries
Vocational Partnerships
The British Council
10 Spring Gardens, London, SW1A 2BN
Tel. 020 7389 4626; Fax. 020 7389 4627
e-mail *vocational.partnerships@britishcouncil.org.*
WWW *http:www.britishcouncil.org/education/vet*

Awarding bodies

There are a great many awarding bodies. Those listed here, between them cover a large proportion of available NVQs. If none of them offers the one you are interested in, you can get the necessary details from QCA, the relevant standards-setting body or NTO.

City and Guilds
1 Giltspur Street, London, EC1A 9DD
Tel. 0207 294 2468; Fax. 0207 294 2400
e-mail *enquiry@city-and-guilds.co.uk*
WWW *http://www.city-and-guilds.co.uk*

Edexcel
Edexcel Foundation, Stewart House
32 Russell Square, London, WC1B 5DN
Tel. 020 7393 4444; Fax. 020 7393 4445
e-mail *enquiries@edexcel.org.uk*
WWW *http://www.edexcel.org.uk*

Scottish Qualifications Authority (SQA)
Hanover House
24 Douglas Street, Glasgow, G2 7NQ
Tel. 0845 279 10000; Fax. 0141 242 2244
e-mail *helpdesk@sqa.org.uk*
WWW *http://www.sqa.org.uk*

Learning and Skills Council

Learning and Skills Council (LSC)
Cheylesmore House
Quinton Road, Coventry, CV1 2WT
Tel. 0845 0194162; Fax. 02476 493600
e-mail *info@isc.gov.uk*
WWW *http://www.isc.gov.uk*

Department for Education and Skills (DfES)
WWW / /*http://www.dfes.gov.uk/section97/*
This site has a useful online database containing information on NVQs. If you click on the 'search for qualifications' button, then tick the 'qualification category' box and select 'NVQs' in the pull down menu that appears, you gain access to a database of links to all current NVQs.

Sector Skills Councils

In the first instance you may obtain the address of the NTO Sector Skills Council, or standards-setting body for your sector, from your local Learning and Skills Council or QCA or SQA. An alternative source of information is Sector Skills Development Agency.

Sector Skills Development Agency
e-mail *ssda.info@dfes.gsi.gov.uk*
WWW *http://www.ssda.org.uk*

Sector Skills Councils will be replacing National Training Organisations. During the transition it would appear – at the time of publication – there will no longer be an easily accessible central listing to include NTOs.

Knowledge to underpin NVQs

Clearly there will be many local colleges and commercial providers able to assist. In terms of countrywide coverage the University for Industry's course provision is marketed as:

learndirect
PO Box 900, Manchester, M60 3LE
Tel. 0800 101901
e-mail enquiries@learndirect.net
WWW *http://www.learndirect.co.uk*

Selected publications

When the first edition of this book was published there were plenty of books for NVQ trainers, but very few for candidates. That is why this book was written. Now, some of the same books are still available but not all have been updated. Even so, some may help to fill any gaps you have in the broader picture. To obtain references for books that have been published on NVQs, look on the Internet at the British Library Web site (www.bl.uk). On the right hand side of the home page you'll find 'Search for catalogue'. Click here. Then click 'British Library Public Catalogue' and finally click 'Search'. You will then be on the page with the search form. Click 'All material'. Carry out two searches:

NVQ and National Vocational Qualifications. Print the results and take titles from this list to your local bookshop or public library. Note: bookshops can only order books in print. Public libraries will sometimes retain books no longer for sale.

Some of the most useful books are those designed to assist candidates taking one specific NVQ. Sometimes they are published by relevant awarding bodies. While these are often available for the mainstream NVQs they are unusual for NVQs with smaller numbers of candidates. Until further information is available from the DfES, this appears to be the single most accessible listing of NVQs.

British Vocational Qualifications (fourth edition), Kogan Page, London, 2001.
Annual directory which, among other things, includes all essential addresses and available NVQs.

The business benefits of NVQs...the employer's story: case studies, Qualifications and Curriculum Authority, 1998.
Provides some excellent insight into successful NVQ schemes run in real companies (free publication).

Portfolio development towards national standards: a guide for candidates/ advisers and assessors, Janice Marshall, Development Processes (Publications) Ltd, 1993.
Obtainable from Development Processes (Publications) Ltd, The Granary, 50 Barton Road, Worsley, Manchester, M28 4PB.

Preparing your NVQ portfolio: A step-by-step guide guide for candidates at levels 1, 2 and 3, Glenn Clarke, Kogan Page, London, 1997.
Provides very detailed guidance on this aspect of an NVQ.

Money to learn: financial help for adults in further education and training, DfES Publication Centre.
Available free from the DfEE Publication Centre at PO Box 5050, Annesley, Nottingham, NG15 0DJ.
Tel. 0845 602 2260: Fax. 0845 603 3360
e-mail *dfee@prolog.uk.com*
WWW *http://www.learndirect.co.uk/advice/helpandadvice/helpwithfunding/*

Note: The Independent Learning Account (ILA) mentioned in this publication has now been abolished.

ABBREVIATIONS AND JARGON

Abbreviations

APA	Accreditation of prior achievement
APL	Accreditation of prior learning
LSC	Learning and Skills Council
NTO	National Training Organization
NVQ	National Vocational Qualification
QCA	Qualifications and Curriculum Authority
SQA	Scottish Qualification Authority
SSC	Sector Skills Council
SSDA	Sector Skills Development Agency
SVQ	Scottish Vocational Qualification
UKU	Underpinning Knowledge and Understanding

Jargon

Accreditation of prior achievement (APA) The assessment and accreditation of existing skills, knowledge and achievements

Accreditation of prior learning (APL) The assessment and accreditation of existing learning, including skills, knowledge and achievements

Assessor Person appointed to carry out judgement of candidate's evidence of competence

Assessment centre Organization, rather than physical location, through which assessment is carried out

Awarding body Organization appointed by standards-setting body and approved by QCA to offer qualifications

Competence The proven ability to work to the national standard for your work

Current (1) Up to date; (2) Even if you acquired the skill some time ago, you still possess it

Element Smallest meaningful activity

Evidence Proof (as in a court of law) of competence

Level Degree of difficulty

Learning and Skills Council (LSC) Regional organization responsible for promotion of training and NVQs. Has national organisation of same name

National Training Organization (NTO) Organization approved as representative of an industrial sector (such as gas or local government) to promote and encourage all aspects of training. Responsible for NVQ development and revision. Forerunner of Sector Skills Council

National Vocational Qualification (NVQ) Competence-based qualification focused on the workplace

Occupational Standards Council Grouping of standards-setting bodies for affiliated sectors. Often being replaced by NTOs

Open access Without, as far as possible, barriers for potential candidates

Outcome Result

Performance Criteria Outcomes required against which candidate's evidence will be assessed

Qualifications and Curriculum Authority (QCA) Body that establishes all requirements and oversees NVQs. Covers England, Wales and Northern Ireland

Range Contexts in which activity must be carried out to prove competence – often integrated within performance and knowledge in new-style NVQs

Scottish Qualifications Authority (SQA) Scottish equivalent of QCA. Has same responsibilities in Scotland for SVQs and has the additional role of an awarding body

Scottish Vocational Qualification (SVQ) Scottish version of the NVQ. Developed from same standards

Sector Skills Council (SSC) During 2002 will start to replace National Training Organizations (NTOs). Among their responsibilities will be promotion of learning and qualifications and improvement in training and standards – including NVQs

Sector Skills Development Agency (SSDA) Set up in April 2002. It will oversee, guide and underpin Sector Skills Councils and provide a Web site through which to access their information

Standards The entire collection of units and elements developed for the preparation of NVQs in a particular occupational area

Standards-setting body Organization responsible for setting occupational standards for a particular sector. These include: SSCs, NTOs, ITOs, OSCs and Lead Bodies

Transferable May be applied in circumstances additional to those in which assessed

Underpinning Knowledge and Understanding (UKU) The theory, principles and understanding essential to competent performance of NVQ units. Sometimes these need assessment additional to the evidence from performance – testing formally or informally

Unit   A group of elements which together comprise a recognizable function. The smallest grouping certificated

Verifier/Moderator   (1) Internal verifier oversees and supports assessor and will often coordinate programme; (2) External verifier is sent from awarding body to oversee and advise assessment centre

WHICH NVQ IS FOR YOU?

This list gives you some idea of the NVQ' s you can take; but bear in mind, for example, the single heading 'Boats and boatbuilding' includes not only 'Boat production', 'Boat maintenance' and 'Boat repair', but also 'Port passenger operations'.

Accountancy and mathematics
Aeronautical and avionic
    engineering
Agricultural/garden machinery
    engineering
Agriculture
Air transport
Amenity horticulture
Animal care
Architectural studies
Armed forces
Art and design
Bakery and confectionery
Beauty
Boats and boatbuilding
Brickwork and masonry
Building
Business studies and services
Care
Carpentry and joinery
Catering and hospitality
Ceramics
Chemical and biochemical
    engineering
Children and child care
Cleaning, laundry and dry
    cleaning
Communications and media
Community work
Computing, information systems
    and technology
Conservation

Construction management
Crafts
Crime investigation and police
    work
Customer services
Demolition
Dentistry
Electrical power and
    electronics
Emergency services
Engineering (general)
Environmental studies
Extracting and providing natural
    resources
Fencing
Film, video and television
Financial services
Fishkeeping and fishing
Floristry
Food and drink
Footwear
Forestry and arboriculture
Funeral services
Furniture and furnishings
Gas supply
Glass technology and glazing
Guidance
Hairdressing
Health and safety
Heating and ventilation
Horticulture
Housing

Human resources and personnel
    management
Information/Library work *
    *Although this is in the new
    Directory, it was dropped by OCR
    in July 2001. No new candidates
    are able to register, although
    existing candidates have until
    2004 to complete their awards.*
Insulation
Insurance
Jewellery
Journalism
Land and countryside studies
Law
Linguistics, languages and
    translation
Maintenance
Management
Manufacturing and design
Manufacturing and designing
Maritime engineering
Mechanical engineering
Medicine
Metals and metalwork
Mining
Museums, galleries and heritage
Music and musical instruments
Office and secretarial
Painting and decorating
Paper and board
Pensions
Performing arts
Petroleum, oil and gas
    technology
Pharmaceutical products
Photography and photographic
    services
Plant operations
Plastering

Plastics and rubber
Plumbing
Printing
Probation and prison work
Process and plant engineering
Process work
Property
Providing business services
Providing goods and services
Providing health, social care and
    protective services
Publishing
Purchasing and supply
Retail
Road works
Roofing
Sales
Scaffolding and rigging
Sciences
Security
Sport, leisure and recreation
Storage and distribution
Surveying
Teaching and training
Technical services
Telecommunications
Tending animals, plants and
    land
Testing/quality control
Textile/crafts/fashion
Tobacco
Town planning
Trains
Transport studies
Travel and tourism
Vehicle maintenance
Waste and refuse
Water treatment and supply
Welding
Woodwork

INDEX

If you cannot find what you want in the index, try looking at the summaries at the start of each chapter.